DATE DUE

DEMCO 38-297

"Flowering Judas"

Women
Writers
Texts and Contexts

VOLUMES IN THE SERIES

"Flowering Judas"

KATHERINE ANNE PORTER ■

Edited, with an introduction by
VIRGINIA SPENCER CARR

Rutgers University Press
New Brunswick, New Jersey

Library of Congress Cataloging-in-Publication Data

Flowering Judas / by Virginia Spencer Carr.
    p.   cm. — (Women writers)
    Includes bibliographical references.
    ISBN 0-8135-1978-0 (cloth) — ISBN 0-8135-1979-9 (paper)
    1. Porter, Katherine Anne, 1890–1980. Flowering Judas. 2. Women
and literature—United States—History—20th century. 3. Mexico in literature. I. Porter, Katherine Anne, 1890–1980. Flowering Judas. 1993.
II. Carr, Virginia Spencer. III. Series: Women writers (New Brunswick,
N.J.)
PS3531.0752F634   1993
813'.52—dc20   92-35362
                                                        CIP

British Cataloging-in-Publication information available

for
Colin Anthony Lee
and Rachel Elizabeth Lee

❏ Contents ■

Contents

❏ Acknowledgments ■

This volume had its nascence with the Katherine Anne Porter Centennial Celebration at Georgia State University in November 1991. That auspicious occasion was made possible by the generous support of Mrs. John B. Amos, the Georgia Humanities Council, and Professor Emeritus Kenneth M. England, Dean Robert L. Arrington, and Provost Thomas J. La Belle of Georgia State University, all of whom I gratefully acknowledge.

I am also grateful to Patricia Bryan and James Poulakos for their assistance in proofreading and preparing the final manuscript, and to Mary Robbins for her help in proofreading my work in this volume.

For the photograph of Porter, I thank Paul Porter, the photographer, and Blanche Ebeling-Koning, curator for many years of Special Collections at the University of Maryland at College Park Libraries, where the photograph resides.

I thank also Connie L. Richards and Thomas L. Erskine, American Women Writers Casebook Series editors; Leslie Mitchner, Executive Editor of Rutgers University Press; and Stuart Mitchner, my copy editor, for their patience, advice, and fine editorial suggestions.

And last, I am deeply appreciative of Rae Carlton Colley, a graduate research assistant in the Department of English at Georgia State University who helped me through every phase of the book, including the selection of the essays, permissions, and the preparation of the final manuscript, all while preparing for her comprehensive examinations and writing her master's thesis, a study of Porter's marginalia. She gave unstintingly of her time and intellect and taught me a great deal about Porter that I did not know.

❏ Introduction

Introduction

"My writing was the only thing that made life worth living,
and having it made everything."
—KATHERINE ANNE PORTER

I

Katherine Anne Porter was a brilliant writer of short fiction. Although her life in Texas as a child and young woman contributed significantly to her emergence as a writer, her apprenticeship dates, essentially, from her twenty-fifth year, when she divorced her husband and began doing the things vital to her self-discovery and growth. She acted; wrote theater reviews and publicity; jotted random observations, impressions, and character sketches; and kept a journal. Upon placing a few free-lance pieces in various newspapers, she began thinking of herself as an investigative reporter. Meanwhile, her understanding of events and people and her distinctive sense of place were intermingling and steeping until she was ready to transmogrify life into fiction. "What you write is a sum of your experience and yourself," Porter insisted.[1]

Her parents named her Callista Russell upon her birth on May 15, 1890, in Indian Creek, Texas, and called her Callie. The next to the youngest of four children, she barely knew her mother, who died at the age of twenty-seven. Her father, Harrison Boone Porter, blamed himself for his wife's death and told his children he wished they had never been born. Callie was not yet two when her father packed them up and took them to Kyle, a small farm community near Austin, so that they could be reared by his widowed mother.

Among her earliest memories was the beating her grandmother gave her when she declared at six that she wanted to be an actress. Actresses were immoral women, and Callie was to have nothing to do with the theater, instructed

her grandmother, whose name—Catharine Anne Porter—
Callie later took for her own, although she slightly changed
the spelling. She was eleven when her grandmother died. Her
memories of her grandmother's wrath and of the nine years
under her strident supervision were grim. Later, as a writer,
she mined the vein of her upbringing, creating from it a fa-
milial world strikingly different from the one she knew first-
hand. Similarly, Porter related to friends that she had grown
up in a privileged family on a sprawling, elegantly furnished
plantation. She also fashioned an elaborate genealogy of dis-
tinguished ancestors. Once created, her imagined characters
took on a life of their own. She never ceased spinning yarns
and making them her reality in any situation. At the same
time, she called her fiction reportage: "Only I do something to
it; I arrange it and it is fiction, but it happened."[2] Her biog-
raphers have tried to distinguish fact from fiction in her work,
but ultimately conclude that she created, by design and necessity, her own version of truth, memory, and imagination. To
those who knew Porter over the years, she remained an incur-
able romantic wanderer whose quest for the ideal relationship—the ideal lover, husband, and friend in a single being—always eluded her.[3]

Porter's formal education was brief. She attended several years of grade school in Kyle before moving to San Antonio to enroll with her older sister Gay at the Thomas School
for Girls, where they took lessons in elocution, voice, dancing,
and drama. After the death of his mother, Harrison Porter contributed little to the upbringing of his children, and before
long they appear to have supported him. At fourteen, Porter—
now calling herself Katherine Russell—moved with her older
sister to Victoria, Texas, to open a school that they advertised
as a "studio of music, physical culture, and dramatic reading."[4] They opened a similar studio a year later in Lufkin,
Texas, but abandoned it shortly, having decided on a new venture: matrimony. The sisters were married in a double ceremony on June 20, 1906. Porter was sixteen and her groom,
John Henry Koontz, also a Texan, twenty-one.

The couple had little in common. Koontz's Roman
Catholic parents disapproved of the union, the civil ceremony
having been conducted by a Methodist minister. They viewed
their daughter-in-law as a flighty and temperamental spend-

thrift. Porter and her husband moved to Houston after he was laid off by Southern Pacific Railway. Working as a wholesale produce clerk, the frugal Koontz saved enough money to build a house in Houston, and for a time Porter seemed happy in the marriage. She converted to Roman Catholicism to please her mother-in-law, who never forgave her for not also giving her a grandchild. In 1912 the couple moved to Corpus Christi, where Porter was reunited with a childhood friend whose contented life with a successful husband, a fine house on the Gulf, a child, and servants all contrasted sharply with her own situation. Two years later, having decided that she had long since stopped loving her husband, Porter set out alone for Chicago, bent once again upon becoming an actress. She managed to secure a few bit parts with a motion picture studio, but there was little about Chicago that appealed to her, and she quickly ran out of money. By year's end, she was back in Texas and living with her sister Gay, now husbandless with two young children to support. To help them, Porter joined a lyceum circuit, dressed in a red medieval outfit, and traveled through western Louisiana and eastern Texas singing Scottish ballads and folk lays and reciting poetry to crowds of country folk in cold, drafty halls. Although Porter relished her flair for the dramatic and loved being on stage, the demands of the lyceum circuit were many, and she grew increasingly frail. Finally, ill with bronchitis, she returned to Dallas to sever formally her nine-year marriage to Koontz and to change her name, legally this time, to *Katherine Porter*.[5]

Elated by her new sense of independence, Porter contemplated the fame and success that she saw as her destiny, but suffered a setback when she came down with tuberculosis. While recuperating in a charity hospital in Dallas, she lived for six months among the destitute and dying. Finally, with the help of her brother Paul, an enlisted man in the Navy, she was moved to Carlsbad Sanatorium in west Texas. There she met Kitty Barry Crawford, who helped her chart her course as a journalist. Even as a young child, Porter had realized that she was adept at language and could use it to her advantage; she had written a few poems and tales while married to Koontz, but not until her meeting Crawford, a career newspaperwoman, had she thought of writing as a profession.

Soon after her release from the hospital, Porter moved

to Fort Worth to write society notes and theater reviews for the *Fort Worth Critic,* a newspaper founded by Crawford and her husband. In the fall of 1918, she moved to Denver to write for the *Rocky Mountain News*. For this move, she paid dearly. When the great influenza epidemic swept across the Rockies and left thousands dead, Porter, too, was striken. Although she was so close to death that her father made arrangements for her burial, an experimental dosage of strychnine administered by a young intern led to her remarkable recovery. Porter was never certain whether it was the illness or the cure that caused her abundant dark curls to fall out, but with the slow growth of new hair, now considerably altered in texture and stark white, she knew that her life had been irrevocably changed.

Subsequent reportage and theater reviews confirmed that her way of looking at events—and at life itself—had undergone a marked change. She became increasingly critical of those who remained neutral in the face of controversial issues and intolerant of those who judged actions and deeds to be intrinsically right or wrong.[6] Meanwhile, during the winter of 1918–1919, Denver's burgeoning Little Theatre brought more realistic plotting and characterization to its stage, whereupon Porter began acting once more, now assured that there were roles for her in which she could be cast as a strong-willed woman of plausible actions. She might have stayed on indefinitely in Denver if her niece Mary Alice Holloway had not died of spinal meningitis during the summer of 1919. It was a death to which she was never reconciled, and it brought to a close her life in the Southwest.

In an attempt to distance herself from her past, Porter settled in New York's Greenwich Village among a coterie of dissenting artists, writers, and political radicals. For a time she drafted publicity for a motion picture studio and, to amuse herself, concocted fairy tales for children that she discovered were marketable. In the three that were published in 1920—"The Shattered Star," "The Faithful Princess," and "The Magic Earring"—Porter gave voice to her evolving feminist leanings. She scoffed at the typical male protagonists and peopled her own mythic terrains with clever and decisive women who handily defeat their unimaginative male adversaries.[7] She also published an adult tale that year, "The Adventures of Hadji: A Tale of a Turkish Coffee-House." An early attempt to clarify her emerging feminism in fiction, its plot turns on the success of a resourceful, aging woman who outwits her female rival and regains the esteem of her husband.[8] All her early stories reveal the same concern for women overcoming difficult circumstances that characterizes her later fiction, wherein the self-worth of her women is measured by their ingenuity in outwitting the men who try to control their lives. It is the women, rather than some omnipotent higher force, who grant absolution—if they choose—to their chastened lovers.[9] For Porter, as with her fictional characters, to act forthrightly was the important thing; merely to stay one's course, to fail to act, meant stagnation and even death.

Despite her successful venture into fiction and a widening circle of literary friends in the Village, Porter was tempted to join the colony of American expatriates in Paris. Meanwhile, however, she had become acquainted with several influential Mexican patriots who assured her that it would be much cheaper to live in Mexico than anywhere in Europe. More to the point, Mexico was changing dramatically, and she should be there to witness it, they insisted. The political situation had been precarious for a decade upon the overthrow of Porfirio Díaz, its dictator-president for thirty-five years. By the fall of 1920, most of the revolutionaries who had hoped to succeed him were dead. Pancho Villa was living in unremarkable retirement in an hacienda in the country, and a new political bandit, Alvaro Obregón, had just won the presidency of Mexico in a sweeping popular vote. Since financing the trip on her own was out of the question, Porter wangled a long-term assignment from the editors of the *Magazine of Mexico*, which was backed by wealthy American bankers interested in their country's official recognition of Obregón's government. Adolpho Best Maugard, a Mexican artist and set designer, prepared letters of introduction for her and lectured her on Aztec and Maya art and the history and folklore of his people.

Finally, given carte blanche for her reporting, Porter set out alone by train from New York City in early November 1920. After crossing the border below San Antonio, the train brimming with Mexican soldiers and their families, she looked out on shells of burned-out buildings, a countryside pocked by cannon fire, farms in ruins, and wary peasants, all in stark relief against the dry hills. In the towns she saw banners and crudely scrawled signs demanding bread, land, and freedom for the country's oppressed Indians and death to tyranny. Politicians, soldiers, bandits, rogues, and revolutionaries contributed to Porter's sudden immersion in international politics and intrigue. In short, everything she saw and heard had an intense effect upon her fiction and, most particularly, upon "Flowering Judas."

Porter's credentials as an American journalist assured her of an invitation to Obregón's inaugural ceremony and the festivities that followed, while Best Maugard's letters introduced her to a new set of friends among the steadily growing community of folk artists. She met labor leaders who vied for her attention and invited her to attend their meetings, and within a few weeks she was conducting dance classes for young women in a technical high school and conveying food and messages to jailed political prisoners. Although she joined the Communist party while living in Mexico City, she renounced her membership when she realized that she was being manipulated dishonestly.[10] Her closest friend was Mary Louise Doherty, who conducted classes in English at a village school for Indian children Porter often visited. Like Laura in "Flowering Judas," Porter received a vicarious pleasure from observing her friend's activities, but without committing herself to the revolution with the zeal of the other activists. On the other hand, determined to experience "all of Mexico and its people," she rode horseback through the countryside, climbed the pyramids, frequented coffee houses where she engaged in seemingly endless talk, and danced late into the night with an assortment of suitors.[11] She also immersed herself in the language, history, and folk art of the people. In short, Porter felt more at home in Mexico at this point than anywhere else she had ever lived.[12]

An accurate observer of people and events, Porter recorded her personal impressions and observations carefully and sent dispatches to the *Magazine of Mexico,* which paid her a modest salary. Given the political uncertainty in Mexico at the time, it was perhaps inevitable that Porter's departure in June 1921 was sudden and unannounced. Activists who had supported Obregón at the polls found themselves accused of treason and branded as fugitives, many being arrested and held prisoner, others summarily executed. Despite having witnessed the suppression of many of Obregón's supporters, she was horrified to learn that her own activities were suspect and that she herself might be arrested or deported.[13] Rather than challenge the rumored allegations, she left the country as quickly and as quietly as possible on a midnight train bound for Dallas.

After a stay in Fort Worth, where she wrote a column for the local paper and acted in almost every play of the local repertory company's 1922–1923 season, Porter returned to Greenwich Village. There she wrote a well-informed political piece based on her Mexican experience called "Where Presidents Have No Friends," which was immediately accepted by Carl Van Doren for the July 1922 issue of *Century*. Recognizing that the article had many characteristics of the short story, a form he was particularly interested in, Van Doren asked for more. It was at this point in her career that Porter decided that the writing of short fiction would be her forte and set about immediately to write her next serious tale, "María Concepción," which depicts an oppressed and uneducated Indian woman who handily turns the tables on her adversaries. After defeating her philandering husband, his mistress, and by extension, the inexorable odds of a male-dominated world, Maria regains her repentant husband as well as the infant of his former mistress, having killed the baby's mother after delivering her own stillborn infant. Porter routinely spoke of "María Concepción" as her "first published story." What she meant was that it was the story that had launched her and the first that was worthy of her name.[14] To many readers, in retrospect, it seemed that Porter's talent had sprung full blown with "María Concepción," which also appeared in *Century*.

Porter returned to Mexico City during the summer of 1922 at the invitation of President Obregón, the circumstances of her sudden departure exactly a year earlier now apparently irrelevant. She had been commissioned to write the copy for an exhibition catalogue for a government-sponsored traveling collection of paintings, sculptures, and popular folk art by young, emerging Mexican artists and to work with her friend Best Maugard and other artists who were helping to assemble it. Although the exhibit was eventually denied entry into the United States because of the administration's opposition to the Obregón regime, Porter's intensive work in preparing the catalogue contributed significantly to her own evolving aesthetic philosophy. During her second sojourn in Mexico, she became a friend of Diego Rivera and helped with the grinding of paints for his huge murals on the interior walls of government buildings. Through her embrace of Mexico's art and culture, Porter realized that she was discovering her own sense of place, as well as the source of much of the fiction she was yet to write. Her developing appreciation of Mexican folk art also contributed to her awareness that the land of the farm people in the simple hill country of southwest Texas—her land—had lain fallow in her creative imagination for far too long.

After returning to New York City in the late summer of 1922, Porter sold two more stories to *Century* that drew upon her Mexican sources ("The Martyr" and "Virgin Violeta") and supported herself writing book reviews for *The New Republic* and the *New York Herald Tribune*. Other than her reviews, Porter published nothing else for three years, having turned from the writing of short stories to a book-length study of Cotton Mather, whose preoccupation with the duality of good and evil mirrored her own. After spending several months in 1927 in Salem, Massachusetts, Porter signed a contract with Horace Liveright for a full-scale biography of Mather, which she anticipated finishing in two years.[15] She progressed fairly well on her Mather project through spurts of writing made possible by retreats to various small guest houses in New England. During one such period of seclusion, she interrupted the biography to write a tale drawing exclusively upon her Mexican sojourn.

Although Porter spoke variously over the years regarding the sources of "Flowering Judas," she said that she knew from the beginning that her protagonist, Laura, was a woman in an alien culture who had an important discovery to make about herself, yet was incapable of making it. Porter admitted to Laura's having been modeled, in part at least, on Mary Doherty, the schoolteacher friend who had once asked Porter to sit with her during a visit by Samuel O. Yúdico, a Mexican labor leader who announced that he was coming to serenade her. Porter said that as she passed Doherty's window that evening she saw something in her friend's face and pose, "something in the whole situation, that set up a commotion" in her mind and contributed to the making of the story.[16]

Porter's realization that it was her own time to act—to write the tale that had gestated for almost a decade—came upon her without warning, as she told it, while she was staying with friends in Brooklyn. She said that she had turned down a bridge game after dinner (the evening of November 29, 1929) and retired to her room with an almost inexplicable sense of urgency. Five hours later she tramped alone through swirling snow to a corner mailbox to post the story to *Hound and Horn*, along with a letter to its managing editor, R. P. Blackmur, describing her tale as "one of a half dozen somewhat in the same vein, with Mexico as the background" that she expected to finish that winter. She asked, also, if she should have attributed the title to T. S. Eliot, having discovered it in his poem "Gerontion." Once the story was accepted, Porter requested early payment. "It occurs to me that you probably pay on publication, and if you do, this would be so sad for me," she began. "I shall ask you to suspend your rule this once in my favor. Existence, in a purely material sense, is for me, I assure you, precarious."[17] Porter's petition may have fallen on sympathetic ears, but policy was policy, and she was paid in the usual manner upon publication the following spring. Six months later, *Flowering Judas and Other Stories* appeared in a limited edition of six hundred copies.

The early reviews of *Flowering Judas and Other Stories* caught up with Porter in Xochimilco, Mexico, where she was living and writing while trying to recover her health after another serious bronchial attack.[18] Critic and poet Louise Bogan informed readers of *The New Republic* that "Flowering Judas" was "startling in its complexity" and the writing "firm and delicate."[19] Bogan implored Porter to "demand much work of her talent," explaining that there was "nothing quite like it, and very little that approaches its strength in contemporary writing." In a review published in *The Nation*, Allen Tate called Porter "a new star" and declared her style "the most economical" and "richest" in American fiction. Whereas some first books are aptly described as "promising," Porter's book "promised nothing," insisted Tate; rather, her work was "a fully matured art."[20] Yvor Winters thought "Flowering Judas" superior to the writings of all other living Americans with one exception: an unnamed short story by William Carlos Williams.[21]

In 1935, upon publication of a new edition of *Flowering Judas and Other Stories*—to which Porter added three additional tales, "The Cracked Looking Glass," "Hacienda," and "That Tree"—reviewers confirmed the original assessments. In the *New York Herald Tribune* she was described as "probably the finest short story writer in America,"[22] while a reviewer for the *New York Times* declared her "indubitably among the most brilliant of our writers of short stories."[23] A review in *Forum and Century* called Porter's style "as subtle and lovely as Kay Boyle's" and found it superior to Boyle's in its "greater vitality and less rarefied mannerisms."[24] Almost all of the reviewers found "Flowering Judas" a perfect, or near perfect, story, regardless of the standard by which it was judged.

By the end of the 1930s, her reputation was reinforced by the publication of a second collection, *Pale Horse, Pale Rider: Three Short Novels* (1939), which included the title work, "Old Mortality," and "Noon Wine." Critics continued to describe her as a prose stylist of the "first rank" and one of the great contemporary American writers.[25] Some compared her fiction favorably to the best stories of Hawthorne, Flaubert, and James, with Glenway Wescott's identifying her as "the sort of writer that we now need: one who maintains standards against which literary excesses and fads may be evaluated"[26] and Robert Penn Warren's encouraging readers to go beyond the fact that she was "justly praised as a stylist" and to note that the "various devices of her prose" always take the reader "to the core meaning of a scene and from there to the theme of the story, which is usually ironical." Implicit in Porter's ironical structure, which Warren described as "irony with a center" (never irony for its own sake), was her "refusal to accept the formula, the ready-made solution."[27] Reviewers of Porter's next collection, *The Leaning Tower and Other Stories* (1944), found that the new stories provided undisputed evidence of dazzling versatility and of her "complete mastery of her medium." Again, she was judged a short story writer "without rival" and the "most flawless realist" of her generation.[28]

In 1941, at the urging of her readers, editors, and publishers, Porter began work on a novel, *Ship of Fools*, for which she signed a contract with Harcourt, Brace. The book had its roots in her transatlantic voyage from Mexico to Germany aboard the *S.S. Werra* in August 1931. After trying first to develop it into a short story, she found her material unwieldy and abandoned the idea until she could shape it into a novel. The book itself evolved so slowly that reviewers and critics began to mention with increasing frequency that her novel was *still* in progress and to speculate upon the date of its eventual publication, observations Porter found annoying.[29] In a letter to James F. Powers in 1967, five years after finally publishing *Ship of Fools*, she referred to "the Novel as an Instrument of Torture. . . . You know, I never had anything against short story writers writing novels, if they wanted to or felt they could, or should. My whole argument was against a short story writer being compelled to write novels when he didn't know how, or wasn't ready.[30]

Although Porter published two additional books of nonfiction (*The Collected Essays and Occasional Writings of Katherine Anne Porter* and *The Never Ending Wrong*) and *The Collected Stories of Katherine Anne Porter* (with three or four new additions), her *Flowering Judas* and *Pale Horse, Pale Rider* volumes marked, essentially, the end of her richest creative period. After that, her literary achievements were more tangibly apparent in other ways. She was the recipient of two Guggenheim fellowships and numerous prizes. She held appointments as a Fellow of the Library of Congress and as Writer in Residence at Stanford University. In 1947 she began giving talks and readings from her fiction and prose writings to hundreds of students in colleges and universities across the country and was awarded a number of honorary degrees. She served as vice-president of the National Institute of Arts and Letters, the second woman to be named an officer of the Institute, which presented her the Gold Medal for Fiction in 1966, the same year she received a National Book Award and Pulitzer Prize for *The Collected Stories of Katherine Anne Porter*.

By this time, scholars, too, had begun to examine closely her work and to write about it critically for publication in refereed journals. She became the subject of many book-length critical studies, theses and dissertations, interviews, a biography, collections of letters and essays, a number of narrowly focused books, and over one hundred fifty critical essays.

II

Porter often spoke of "Flowering Judas" as the tale she liked best of all that she had written because it came "very near" to what she meant it to be. "An author's choice of his own work must always be decided by such private knowledge of the margin between intention and the accomplished fact," she explained.[31] In her introduction to Eudora Welty's first book, *A Curtain of Green and Other Stories,* Porter described the kind of story she preferred as "one in which external act and the internal voiceless life of the human imagination almost meet and mingle on the mysterious threshold between dream and waking, one reality refusing to admit or confirm the other, yet both conspiring toward the same end."[32]

"Flowering Judas" is such a story. Laura, the protagonist, travels to Mexico at the age of twenty-two much as Porter herself did at thirty-one, to "attend and assist" the Obregón Revolution.[33] Life in Mexico City in 1921 and everything associated with the revolution—the atmosphere, ideas, and new friends—are as true for the fictional Laura as they were for Porter, who described her intimates in Mexico as "almost pure revolutionaries" who fed her dissenting nature. "I was involved in that atmosphere. I was drawn into it like the girl [Laura] who took messages to people living in dark alleys. . . . But I'm not the girl entirely." It was Mary Doherty whom the "fat revolutionist with a guitar" visited regularly. Porter spoke of Doherty as "one of those virtuous, intact, strait-laced Irish Catholic girls" who had no real knowledge of "how to take care of herself."[34]

At the onset of the tale, Laura has been in Mexico for several months. Just how many is unclear, but it has been long enough for her to become useful to the revolutionists, who trust her, albeit they find her "full of romantic error." By employing the present tense and establishing a unity of time and place—a single evening in Laura's apartment—Porter creates at once a sense of immediacy. Most of what one learns about Laura and her unwelcome visitor is revealed in flashback.

Exposition, dialogue, interior thoughts, omniscient inferences, reported actions and events, Laura's disturbing dream, and an even more troubling awakening combine effectively to bring the story to closure.

Porter's use of the passive voice through her omniscient narrator is crucial to the characterization and events of the tale. It also enables Porter to maintain her own aesthetic distance from Laura, who "cannot help feeling that she has been betrayed irreparably by the disunion between her way of living and her feeling of what life should be." Furthermore, Laura is "almost contented to rest in this sense of grievance as a private store of consolation." Although she thinks occasionally of running away, she has no real intention of leaving Mexico; for Laura, Mexico is home. When she longs to "fly out of this room, down the narrow stairs, and into the street where the houses lean together like conspirators . . . and leave Braggioni singing to himself," she thinks only of running away from that which jars her complacency, never *to* something for which she might yearn. Yet she dares not. In effect, she continues to do what she most condemns in Braggioni: she sings an aria of self-delusion. She is the passive participant in the evening's events, just as she has been, typically, throughout her stay in Mexico. "Flowering Judas" is an early and significant testament to Porter's own rejection of passivity and of her commitment to responsible action.

One of the few assertive acts in Laura's past was traveling to Mexico from her home in Arizona to offer her services to the revolution. Although she unwittingly serves as a catalyst for the decisive acts of others, she neither initiates an action nor wishes to be held accountable for one. Saying *no* requires neither engagement nor commitment, and she has made an art of such negation. Like Porter, however, who found that "without knowing it, we are sometimes half in love with evil and don't stop it because it adds color and excitement to life," Laura is enamored of the paradoxical dimensions of good and evil. She pays lip service to innocence, yet trifles with self-knowledge, worldliness, and evil, knowing full well that she will ultimately reject them. Although she regrets her occasional lapses, she views them stoically as antidotes against more threatening encounters. Porter, on the other hand, once declared: "I was not a worldly person, but I was of this world in the sense that I wanted to touch, smell, see, and be. I didn't figure it out. I just did it."[35]

Laura, too, is a rebel, but her protestations are safely subterranean. She wears blue serge and round, white, nun-like collars—"the uniform of an idea"—but she will not renounce the hand-worked lace that she wears daily on her collars. Were her "private heresy" to be known to her "special group" for whom the "sacred" machine is the "salvation of the workers," she would be excommunicated. A Roman Catholic since birth, Laura has "encased herself in a set of principles derived from her early training," and she considers not wearing machine-made lace one such principle. Attending mass regularly is another, but the act of slipping furtively "now and again into some crumbling church" and kneeling "on the chilly stone" to say a "Hail Mary" is "no good." The dying church seems emblematic of the failure of the revolution to alter appreciably the life of the people. For Laura personally, neither her Roman Catholic upbringing nor her high-minded revolutionary ideals can sustain her. Porter juxtaposes the idea of salvation through revolution against salvation through the church in such a way that the reader doubts that either can survive. Both have gone astray through treachery, dishonesty, and misplaced values.

Laura wants to be taken seriously as a revolutionist, yet at every turn she is reminded that a revolution provides a career only for men with skill and high energy who wish to lead. Women may be bearers of food, messages, money, narcotics, sex; they may clean pistols and load amunition belts; they may teach schoolchildren to sing and dance and draw. But they may not be revolutionists. Their roles have been conceived by men and confirmed by history, and these roles are responsive, not initiatory. Laura's most obvious antagonist, Braggioni, commands a large body of men who live in their leader's reflected glow, who speak of his nobility and of his love of humanity that transcends more personal attachments, and who, ultimately, fear for their very lives. Similarly, Laura is expected to bask in his favor and to receive him with the same "tenderness, amplitude, and eternal charity" that he manifests toward himself. She affords him every courtesy, but in her interior life she feels that she is trapped in a nightmare. She envies Braggioni's wife for her opportunities to be alone "to weep as much as she pleases about a concrete wrong." Laura has no such freedom.

One complicating factor is that Porter has made Braggioni so repulsive that readers are tempted to view Laura more sympathetically than she may deserve. Consequently, at the story's end, the fall from grace she has brought upon herself seems all the more horrifying. The tale's opening lines establish its dynamics. Braggioni is slouched in a "straight-back chair much too small for him" while he awaits Laura—his prey, in a sense—in an upper room of her apartment. She has just come in for the evening and wishes to be alone, to undress, undo her hair, and lie down quietly for a few moments before dinner. Everything about her is as tidy, diminutive, and understated as Braggioni, with all his vainglorious bulk, is grotesquely and extravagantly distorted. She sits at a small table, dines quickly upon a modest meal of rice and hot chocolate, then sinks into a deep chair before him. Their routine is established. If he has a new song, he will sing it; if not, she will request something else. Laura listens to Braggioni's songs with "pitiless courtesy" in dramatic contrast to his passionate intensity; and thus she has suffered nightly for a month, having accepted that she "owes her comfortable existence and her salary to him." When he tells her that he might even forgive her for being a *gringita,* she imagines herself wiping the smile from his face with a "sound back-handed slap," but she makes no such move. He seems oblivious to the sudden color in her cheeks or the anger in her eyes, and she is reminded that her "tenacious" resistance must be imperceptible always.

Before the onset of Braggioni's courtship, Laura has deftly rejected two other suitors. One, a young captain in Zapata's army, had "attempted, during a horseback ride near Cuernavaca, to express his desire for her with the noble simplicity befitting a rude folk-hero," but her horse had shied and bolted, followed by the captain's horse, and the potential moment of embrace was lost forever. She tried "to forgive herself for having spurred her horse at the wrong moment," but when he asked her to ride with him again, she "remembered that she must return to Mexico City at noon." Although Laura provokes her adversaries, she makes no attempt to engage them in meaningful action. Rather, she is the one acted upon. Her other suitor, a nineteen-year-old organizer of the Typographers Union, had appeared in her patio one night and serenaded her "like a lost soul for two hours," and upon the advice of her servant she had tossed him a flower. Consequently, the youth had commenced with "all propriety" to court her in accord with convention. Night after night he sang to her; day after day he followed her "at a fixed distance" as she walked the city. He composed love poems, printed them on a wooden press, and attached them to her door. In vain he awaited her response. Although Laura confesses to herself that she should never have thrown the flower, she refuses to regret it. Instead, such "negation of all external events as they occur is a sign that she is gradually perfecting herself in the stoicism she strives to cultivate against that disaster she fears" but cannot name. In effect, she gathers the poisonous flowers and draws them unto her bosom, then strews them in her path to trip up others who dare to follow.

Similarly, she has accepted Braggioni, yet chafes at the tableau in which she appears to be the willing participant. Having rejected love from any source, having never dared to share her intimate being with another, having immunized herself against any assailant, Laura is one of the damned, yet with her limited self-awareness, the reality of her situation is lost to her. Two events of the evening confirm this: the death of Eugenio, the political prisoner to whom she brought narcotics, and her dream later. She had told Braggioni, after oiling and loading his pistols, that she found Eugenio that afternoon going into a stupor because he had taken an overdose of the tablets she had brought him. Moreover, he refused to allow her to summon the prison doctor. "He said he took them because he was bored," she explains. "He is a fool, and death is his own business. We are well rid of him," replies Braggioni. So, too, might he have spoken of Laura.

Meanwhile, the grief-stricken wife he had abandoned during his month-long courtship of Laura has wept nightly and torn her hair. Whe he finally returns to her that evening, the penitent Mrs. Braggioni receives him without reproach. She calls him "angel" and kneels before him and bathes his feet. In a great torrent of tears she begs his forgiveness;

Braggioni weeps, too. He tells her that he is tired and hungry and suggests that they eat something together. Braggioni, concludes Porter's omniscient narrator, "is refreshed by the solemn, endless rain" of his wife's tears, and thus their antici- pated communion—a partaking of the sacrament, as it were, a communion between mere mortals—offers hope for the mo- ment, and it is enough.

Meanwhile Laura has gone to bed and is fighting wake- fulness. "How monstrous" it is to "confuse love with revolu- tion, night with day, life with death—ah, Eugenio!" she cries. Thus invoked, Eugenio, the prisoner who has committed sui- cide, comes to her in a dream upon the tolling of the midnight hour. Whereas she had felt "bogged down" in a nightmare that evening while Braggioni was physically present, Laura now rises "without fear" and follows Eugenio to the "new coun- try . . . far away" to which he leads her. This time, it is he who refuses when she insists that he grasp her hand and lead her. "Then eat these flowers, poor prisoner," he tells her "in a voice of pity." She eats greedily of the "warm bleeding flowers" that he has stripped from the Judas tree in her yard, for they "sat- isfy both hunger and thirst"; but she will not accept that they are his body and his blood, nor will she tolerate his accusatory "Murderer! . . . Cannibal!" Unwilling to accept responsibility for her actions, unwilling to look upon her fellow man and to speak, like Eugenio, "in a voice of pity," Laura is damned to a state of suspension between illusion and reality. Having "en- cased herself in a set of principles derived from her early train- ing," having been the instrument of Eugenio's death, and having eaten, ultimately, of the Judas tree, Laura is both the betrayed and the betrayer. Whereas she had routinely dealt with Braggioni with "pitiless courtesy" and was herself the re- cipient of Eugenio's "voice full of pity," she rejects pity as an emblem of weakness, just as she sees Braggioni as an emblem of her disillusionment. The prisoner Eugenio, who gains his freedom through death, changes places, in effect, with Laura, whom he addresses as "poor prisoner" when he invites her to partake of the Eucharist. Although she does so, she rejects it instantly and awakens "trembling" at the "sound of her own voice." Having denied her humanity, Laura discovers too late the reality of her "uneasy premonitions of the future."

III

Besides the story itself, *Flowering Judas* includes Porter's own statement about the writing of "Flowering Judas," two related essays by her, an interview conducted by Barbara Thompson for the *Paris Review,* and seven critical essays that constitute a wide range of Porter scholarship devoted exclusively to "Flowering Judas."

The *Paris Review* interview is particularly important to Porter scholarship not only because it is one of the few occasions during which Porter answered questions at length about herself, her craft, her methods, and the influences on her writing, but also because it is an artistic, literary piece in itself. Porter's tendency to fictionalize aspects of her past has been noted, especially, by Thomas F. Walsh, whose essay appears in this volume, and Joan Givner. Porter takes liberties with her history in this interview as well, claiming, for example, a distant relationship to Daniel Boone, a connection she later recanted. Of particular interest, of course, is the information regarding the genesis and gestation of "Flowering Judas."

Analytical criticism of "Flowering Judas" began in earnest in 1947 with Ray B. West, Jr.'s "Katherine Anne Porter: Symbol and Theme in 'Flowering Judas,'" which groups the symbols into three general areas or "fields": religious (invoking Christian ideology); secular ("machine-linked" and invoking Marxist ideology); and symbols of love (erotic, secular, or divine). Based on his analysis of the symbolic interactions of the three, West concludes that orthodox religion and Marxist socialism are sterile unless joined by love. Love is impossible if it springs either from formal religion—in this case, Roman Catholicism—or socialism; consequently, Laura denies the necessity of love and is not redeemed. Braggioni embraces love, and for him, redemption is never an issue. Eugenio, a Christ figure, is betrayed by Laura, a Judas figure. Porter herself insisted that she never consciously took or adopted a symbol in her life; she said, for example, that it did not occur to her to entitle the story "Flowering Judas" until she had finished writing it, whereupon she "suddenly saw the whole symbolic plan and pattern" of which she had been "totally unconscious" during the writing itself.[36] Subsequent criticism of "Flowering Judas" draws heavily upon West's essay.

Leon Gottfried's "Death's Other Kingdom: Dantesque and Theological Symbolism in 'Flowering Judas,'" published in 1969 in *PMLA,* marks the introduction of detailed theological criticism and is another essay to which subsequent critics often refer. Gottfried sees "Flowering Judas" as a portrayal of a spiritual hell with no accompanying portrayal of heaven. He believes that Porter herself faced the struggle of the modern Promethean artist who tries to carve some semblance of order from chaos, and he refutes the commonly held view of Eugenio as a Christ figure.

In "The Charged Image in Katherine Anne Porter's 'Flowering Judas'" (1970), David Madden convincingly examines the complexity of Porter's imagery both figuratively and visually, comparing "Flowering Judas" to other genres of art, particularly dance, poetry, and cinema. He views the static quality of these auxiliary images as evidence of Laura's state of mind, a self-delusion that produces paralysis of will. Madden suggests that the images contain thematic implications of denial, rejection of love, and a blurring of the line between reality and illusion.

Darlene Harbour Unrue's essay is a revised excerpt from her book *Truth and Vision in Katherine Anne Porter's Fiction* (1985), an excellent feminist reading of Porter's work in its entirety. Unrue interprets Porter's world view as a search for truth through the vehicle of fiction. Like Jane Krause DeMouy, whose essay follows, she applies Jungian archetypes to "Flowering Judas," exploring the loss of illusion that both Laura and Porter experience in revolutionary Mexico—a loss that directly affects their search for veracity. But while DeMouy suggests that Laura betrays herself by denying her very femininity, Unrue argues that Porter does not intend to portray a frigid or sexually repressed Laura; rather, Laura represses love and sexuality out of a sense of practicality. In describing Laura's "female principle" as a series of Jungian archetypes, Unrue notes that flowers and trees, by their vegetative fertility, represent traditional female virtues. These symbolic principles are united effectively in the symbol of the Judas tree with its "bleeding flowers" and Christian images of betrayal.

Jane Krause DeMouy's essay draws on her book, *Katherine Anne Porter's Women: The Eye of Her Fiction* (1983), the first feminist treatment of Porter's oeuvre, and a fine one. She contends that with the exception of "Noon Wine" and "The Leaning Tower," the central conflict in each work is the struggle of the female protagonist to reconcile her attempts to achieve personal freedom with the Jungian "Great Mother" archetype inherent in all women. The essay reprinted here includes a portion of DeMouy's chapter entitled "The Mirror Image: Virgin and Mother," a duality precisely describing the author's view of Laura's psychosexual position. DeMouy contends that if the reader is to understand Laura's duality, he/she must understand the difficulty women face, and have traditionally faced, in their attempt to achieve some sense of personal freedom and power.

One of the most important recent studies is Thomas F. Walsh's "The Making of 'Flowering Judas,'" which provides background information about the Mexican revolution and the role of Mexico's revolutionaries, labor leaders, politicians, and other participants of the revolution, and, most especially, the rise of Alvaro Obregón; it should be particularly useful to scholars who know Porter's work but are relatively unfamiliar with Mexican history and culture during the first thirty years of the twentieth century. Walsh also breaks new ground in addressing the controversy pertaining to Mary Doherty as the model for Laura.

Previously unpublished, Robert Brinkmeyer's "Mexico, Memory, and Betrayal: Katherine Anne Porter's 'Flowering Judas'" addresses the concerns of many readers who need to understand something more of the Mexican culture from which Porter's story grew. Whereas Walsh deals with the historical genesis of "Flowering Judas," Brinkmeyer examines Mexican art of the early twentieth century, particularly the Indian primitivism that fascinated Porter, who also was distressingly aware of the neglect of Mexico's Indian artists by expatriates. In addition, Brinkmeyer explores the effects of Porter's own psychological struggles upon her protagonist's asceticism, which derive in part from Laura's inability to reconcile her Catholic upbringing with her revolutionary present.

Porter herself was a spirited independent woman all of her life. Some would call her a feminist, but not in the sense by which feminists are known today. Save for gender alone, for example, she refused to identify with the women depicted

in Simone de Beauvoir's *The Second Sex*. In 1962, at the age
of seventy-two, she informed a book reviewer for the *New York
Herald Tribune* that she had little use for books that make
such sweeping assertions as "women are . . . women do . . .
women think."[37] She said that she had never blamed her difficult life on anyone else, nor did she think that being a woman
had ever put her at a disadvantage in a male-dominated culture. Being a woman was exciting, she acknowledged, but
reading about women as women bored her. Porter was an unlikely feminist both in her refusal to join any group and in her
personal distaste for lesbianism, which she associated with the
early feminist movement. Moreover, the very act of aligning
herself with others violated the spirit of individuality on which
she prided herself. When asked by Barbara Thompson about
"choosing a pattern" for her life, Porter replied: "The thing is
not to follow a pattern. . . . The thing is to accept your own life
and not try to live someone else's life. Look, the thumbprint is
not like any other, and the thumbprint is what you must go
by."[38] She went on to say that she had "never belonged to any
group or huddle of any kind." Most of Porter's female protagonists find that family ties, marriage, and love are threats
to their personal freedom, and that a woman must be alone to
be free. Laura, too, lives by such a dictum, but her independence is achieved at great cost. Her only escape from Mexico's
patriarchal society can come through an inner withdrawal
from life, a withdrawal that offers autonomy without hope.
Laura's unwillingness to take chances and her determination
to engage neither enemy nor suitor and to make of her one
positive act a negative is, in effect, to go to bed with the
damned. Porter's own *"En avant!"* was both prayer and battle
cry, and it sustained her for ninety years. She died on September 18, 1980, in Silver Spring, Maryland.

☐ *Notes* ■

1. Joan Givner, ed., (Jackson: University of Mississippi Press,
1987), 13.

2. Joan Givner, "Her Great Art, Her Sober Craft," *Southwest
Review* 63 (Summer 1977): 217.

3. Cleanth Brooks to Virginia Spencer Carr, Oxford, England, 8 March 1992.

4. Joan Givner, *Katherine Anne Porter: A Life,* revised ed. (Athens: University of Georgia Press, 1991), 88.

5. According to Joan Givner, Porter filed for divorce on May 20, 1915; the divorce was granted on June 21st in the name of *Katherine Porter.* Porter added the *Anne,* her grandmother's middle name, unofficially, and publicly, when she began to publish. Years later, after Porter's fourth marriage and divorce, a reporter asked her about a rumored "hidden marriage." She replied that she had never concealed any of her marriages, albeit she might have let one slip her mind occasionally (Givner, *A Life,* 111, 524).

6. See Givner, *A Life,* 134–135. A pervasive theme in Porter's novel, *Ship of Fools,* published in 1962, was an elaboration of her long-standing belief in the passive promotion of evil by innocent people.

7. Givner, *A Life,* 144.

8. "Adventures of Hadji: A Tale of a Turkish Coffee-House," retold by Katherine Anne Porter, *Asia* (August 1920): 683–684. The tale does not appear in any collection of Porter's work.

9. Joan Givner attributes the themes of her subject's early tales to a "marked, and probably unconscious, feminist bias" (*A Life,* 145).

10. Cleanth Brooks to Virginia Spencer Carr, Oxford, 10 March 1992.

11. Brooks interview, 10 March 1992.

12. Paul Porter to Virginia Spencer Carr, Austin, Texas, 5 June 1991.

13. Givner, *A Life,* 156–157; see, also, Thomas F. Walsh, "The Making of Flowering Judas," this volume.

14. Givner, *A Life,* 163.

15. Porter's biography of Cotton Mather remains unpublished except for the three chapters in *The Collected Essays and Occasional Writings of Katherine Anne Porter* (Boston: Houghton Mifflin/Seymour Lawrence, 1970, repr. 1990), 313–351.

16. Barbara Thompson, "Katherine Anne Porter: An Interview," *Writers at Work: The Paris Review Interviews, Second Series* (New York: The Viking Press, 1963), 153–154. Reprinted in this volume.

17. Mitzi Berger Hamovitch, "Today and Yesterday: Letters From Katherine Anne Porter," *The Centennial Review* 38 (Fall 1983): 280.

18. Porter's third visit to Mexico was her longest. She stayed

from late April of 1930 until August 22, 1931, when she sailed from Veracruz to Bremerhaven, Germany.

19. Louise Bogan, "Flowering Judas" (review), *New Republic* 64 (22 October 1930): 278.

20. Allen Tate, "A New Star," *The Nation* 31 (1 October 1930): 353.

21. Yvor Winters, "Major Fiction," *Hound and Horn* 4 (January–March 1931): 303.

22. Eda Lou Walton, "An Exquisite Story-Teller," *New York Herald Tribune Books*, 3 November 1935, 7.

23. Ralph Thompson, "Books of the Times," *New York Times*, 30 January 1937, 15.

24. Edith H. Walton, *"Flowering Judas" and Other Stories*, (review), *Forum and Century* 94 (December 1935): 9.

25. Philip T. Hartung, *"Pale Horse, Pale Rider,* by Katherine Anne Porter, A Review," *Commonweal* 30 (19 May 1939): 109–110.

26. Glenway Wescott, "Praise," *Southern Review* 5 (Summer 1939): 161.

27. Robert Penn Warren, "Katherine Anne Porter (Irony with a Center)," *Kenyon Review* 4 (Winter 1942): 29–42.

28. Vernon A. Young, "The Art of Katherine Anne Porter," *New Mexico Quarterly Review* 15 (August 1945): 326.

29. Isabel Bayley, ed., *Letters of Katherine Anne Porter* (New York: Atlantic Monthly Press, 1990), 610–611.

30. Bayley, *Letters*, 510–511.

31. Katherine Anne Porter, "Why She Selected 'Flowering Judas,'" in *This Is My Best*, ed. Whit Burnett (New York: Dial Press, 1942), 539–540.

32. Katherine Anne Porter, "Introduction," *A Curtain of Green and Other Stories*, by Eudora Welty (New York: Harcourt Brace, 1941), xxi.

33. Givner, *Conversations*, 40. On another occasion Porter admitted to having gone to Mexico to "to build a revolutionary tomorrow with organizers of the labor movement."

34. Givner, *Conversations*, 123.

35. Givner, *Conversations*, 41.

36. Thompson, *Writers at Work*, 137–163.

37. Katherine Anne Porter to Maurice Dolbier, *New York Herald Tribune Books*, 1 April 1962: 3.

38. Thompson, *Writers at Work*, 149.

❏ Chronology ∎

1890   Born Callista Russell Porter in Indian Creek, Texas, May 15.

1892   After mother's death, moves with father and siblings to Kyle, Texas, to be reared by his mother.

1906   Marries John Henry Koontz in Methodist ceremony, June 20.

1911   Converts to Roman Catholicism.

1915   Divorces Koontz and has named changed legally to *Katherine Porter.*

1918   Moves to Denver to write for *Rocky Mountain News;* nearly dies of influenza.

1919   Moves to New York City and begins writing children's stories.

1920   Publishes four short stories; travels to Mexico City in September; meets President Obregón and sends dispatches to *Magazine of Mexico* and *Christian Science Monitor;* returns to Fort Worth in June 1921 when threatened with deportation or arrest.

1922   Makes brief, second trip to Mexico upon appointment by Obregón to help organize the Travelling Mexican Popular Arts Exposition, for which she writes *An Outline of Mexican Popular Arts and Crafts;* returns to New York.

1925   Marries Ernest Stock, an Englishman, in New York (they divorce in 1928).

1927   Signs contract with Boni and Liveright for biography of Cotton Mather and goes to Essex Institute in Salem, Massachusetts, to research and write; protests death sentence for Sacco and Vanzetti in Boston; is arrested, along with John Dos Passos, Edna St. Vincent Millay, Dorothy Parker, and others.

1930   Publishes "Flowering Judas"; sails to Mexico on *S.S. Havana;* publishes first book: *Flowering Judas and Other Stories.*

1931 Is awarded Guggenheim Fellowship in February; sails from Veracruz on August 22 to Bremerhaven, Germany, on *S.S. Werra;* keeps log of crossing, which become basis of *Ship of Fools.*

1933 Marries Eugene Pressly, whom she met in Mexico in 1930; lives in Paris.

1936 Separates from Pressly and returns to New York.

1938 Receives second Guggenheim fellowship; divorces Pressly and marries Albert Erskine (they divorce in 1942).

1939 Publishes *Pale Horse, Pale Rider.*

1940 Spends summer at Yaddo Artists Colony in Sarasota Springs, New York.

1941 Elected to membership in American Institute of Arts and Letters.

1942 Death of father; moves in fall to farmhouse in Ballston Spa, New York.

1944 Is appointed Fellow of the Library of Congress; publishes *The Leaning Tower and Other Stories.*

1945 Moves to Hollywood to collaborate on two films for MGM and Paramount.

1952 Gives opening address at International Exposition of the Arts in Paris; publishes *The Days Before* (Harcourt, Brace).

1954 Begins year-long Fulbright lectureship at University of Liege in Belgium, but is forced by illness to return to New York at end of first semester.

1955 Moves to Southbury, Connecticut, where she lives for three years; death of Paul Porter, her brother.

1962 Publishes *Ship of Fools,* which earns a million dollars; receives Emerson-Thoreau Gold Medal from American Academy of Arts & Sciences in Boston.

1966 Publishes *The Collected Stories of Katherine Anne Porter;* receives National Book Award and Pulitzer Prize; awarded Gold Medal for Fiction from National Institute and Academy of Arts and Letters "for lifetime achievement."

1967 Publishes *A Christmas Story.*

1970 Publishes *The Collected Essays and Occasional Writings of Katherine Anne Porter.*

1974 Orders pine coffin from mail-order carpentry shop in Arizona; delights in opening closet and showing coffin to unsuspecting visitors by stepping into it.

1977 Publishes *The Never-Ending Wrong* to mark exoneration of Sacco and Vanzetti on fiftieth year of their executions.

1980 Dies on September 18 at Carriage Hall Nursing Center, Silver Spring, Maryland.

Flowering Judas

☐ Flowering Judas

Braggioni sits heaped upon the edge of a straight-backed chair much too small for him, and sings to Laura in a furry, mournful voice. Laura has begun to find reasons for avoiding her own house until the latest possible moment, for Braggioni is there almost every night. No matter how late she is, he will be sitting there with a surly, waiting expression, pulling at his kinky yellow hair, thumbing the strings of his guitar, snarling a tune under his breath. Lupe the Indian maid meets Laura at the door, and says with a flicker of a glance toward the upper room, "He waits."

Laura wishes to lie down, she is tired of her hair-pins and the feel of her long tight sleeves, but she says to him, "Have you a new song for me this evening?" If he says yes, she asks him to sing it. If he says no, she remembers his favorite one, and asks him to sing it again. Lupe brings her a cup of chocolate and a plate of rice, and Laura eats at the small table under the lamp, first inviting Braggioni, whose answer is always the same: "I have eaten, and besides, chocolate thickens the voice."

Laura says, "Sing, then," and Braggioni heaves himself into song. He scratches the guitar familiarly as though it were a pet animal, and sings passionately off

---

From *Flowering Judas and Other Stories* by Katherine Anne Porter (New York: Harcourt, Brace, 1930).

key, taking the high notes in a prolonged painful
squeal. Laura, who haunts the markets listening to the
ballad singers, and stops every day to hear the blind boy
playing his reed-flute in Sixteenth of September Street,
listens to Braggioni with pitiless courtesy, because she
dares not smile at his miserable performance. Nobody
dares to smile at him. Braggioni is cruel to everyone,
with a kind of specialized insolence, but he is so vain of
his talents, and so sensitive to slights, it would require a
cruelty and vanity greater than his own to lay a finger
on the vast cureless wound of his self-esteem. It would
require courage, too, for it is dangerous to offend him,
and nobody has this courage.

Braggioni loves himself with such tenderness and
amplitude and eternal charity that his followers—for he
is a leader of men, a skilled revolutionist, and his skin
has been punctured in honorable warfare—warm
themselves in the reflected glow, and say to each other:
"He has a real nobility, a love of humanity raised above
mere personal affections." The excess of this self-love
has flowed out, inconveniently for her, over Laura, who,
with so many others, owes her comfortable situation
and her salary to him. When he is in a very good hu-
mor, he tells her, "I am tempted to forgive you for being
a *gringa. Gringita!*" and Laura, burning, imagines herself leaning forward suddenly, and with a sound back-
handed slap wiping the suety smile from his face. If he
notices her eyes at these moments he gives no sign.

She knows what Braggioni would offer her, and
she must resist tenaciously without appearing to resist,
and if she could avoid it she would not admit even to
herself the slow drift of his intention. During these long
evenings which have spoiled a long month for her, she
sits in her deep chair with an open book on her knees,
resting her eyes on the consoling rigidity of the printed

page when the sight and sound of Braggioni singing threaten to identify themselves with all her remembered afflictions and to add their weight to her uneasy premonitions of the future. The gluttonous bulk of Braggioni has become a symbol of her many disillusions, for a revolutionist should be lean, animated by heroic faith, a vessel of abstract virtues. This is nonsense, she knows it now and is ashamed of it. Revolution must have leaders, and leadership is a career for energetic men. She is, her comrades tell her, full of romantic error, for what she defines as cynicism in them is merely "a developed sense of reality." She is almost too willing to say, "I am wrong, I suppose I don't really understand the principles," and afterward she makes a secret truce with herself, determined not to surrender her will to such expedient logic. But she cannot help feeling that she has been betrayed irreparably by the disunion between her way of living and her feeling of what life should be, and at times she is almost contented to rest in this sense of grievance as a private store of consolation. Sometimes she wishes to run away, but she stays. Now she longs to fly out of this room, down the narrow stairs, and into the street where the houses lean together like conspirators under a single mottled lamp, and leave Braggioni singing to himself.

Instead she looks at Braggioni, frankly and clearly, like a good child who understands the rules of behavior. Her knees cling together under sound blue serge, and her round white collar is not purposely nun-like. She wears the uniform of an idea, and has renounced vanities. She was born Roman Catholic, and in spite of her fear of being seen by someone who might make a scandal of it, she slips now and again into some crumbling little church, kneels on the chilly stone, and says a Hail Mary on the gold rosary she bought in

Tehuantepec. It is no good and she ends by examining
the altar with its tinsel flowers and ragged brocades, and
feels tender about the battered doll-shape of some male
saint whose white, lace-trimmed drawers hang limply
around his ankles below the hieratic dignity of his velvet robe. She has encased herself in a set of principles
derived from her early training, leaving no detail of gesture or of personal taste untouched, and for this reason
she will not wear lace made on machines. This is her
private heresy, for in her special group the machine is
sacred, and will be the salvation of the workers. She
loves fine lace, and there is a tiny edge of fluted cobweb
on this collar, which is one of twenty precisely alike,
folded in blue tissue paper in the upper drawer of her
clothes chest.

Braggioni catches her glance solidly as if he had
been waiting for it, leans forward, balancing his paunch
between his spread knees, and sings with tremendous
emphasis, weighing his words. He has, the song relates,
no father and no mother, nor even a friend to console
him; lonely as a wave of the sea he comes and goes,
lonely as a wave. His mouth opens round and yearns
sideways, his balloon cheeks grow oily with the labor
of song. He bulges marvelously in his expensive garments. Over his lavender collar, crushed upon a purple
necktie, held by a diamond hoop: over his ammunition
belt of tooled leather worked in silver, buckled cruelly
around his gasping middle: over the tops of his glossy
yellow shoes Braggioni swells with ominous ripeness,
his mauve silk hose stretched taut, his ankles bound
with the stout leather thongs of this shoes.

When he stretches his eyelids at Laura she notes
again that his eyes are the true tawny yellow cat's eyes.
He is rich, not in money, he tells her, but in power, and
this power brings with it the blameless ownership of

things, and the right to indulge his love of small luxuries. "I have a taste for the elegant refinements," he said once, flourishing a yellow silk handkerchief before her nose. "Smell that? It is Jockey Club, imported from New York." Nonetheless he is wounded by life. He will say so presently. "It is true everything turns to dust in the hand, to gall on the tongue." He sighs and his leather belt creaks like a saddle girth. "I am disappointed in everything as it comes. Everything." He shakes his head. "You, poor thing, you will be disappointed too. You are born for it. We are more alike than you realize in some things. Wait and see. Some day you will remember what I have told you, you will know that Braggioni was your friend."

Laura feels a slow chill, a purely physical sense of danger, a warning in her blood that violence, mutilation, a shocking death, wait for her with lessening patience. She has translated this fear into something homely, immediate, and sometimes hesitates before crossing the street. "My personal fate is nothing, except as the testimony of a mental attitude," she reminds herself, quoting from some forgotten philosophic primer, and is sensible enough to add, "Anyhow, I shall not be killed by an automobile if I can help it.

"It may be true I am as corrupt, in another way, as Braggioni," she thinks in spite of herself, "as callous, as incomplete," and if this is so, any kind of death seems preferable. Still she sits quietly, she does not run. Where could she go? Uninvited she has promised herself to this place; she can no longer imagine herself as living in another country, and there is no pleasure in remembering her life before she came here.

Precisely what is the nature of this devotion, its true motives, and what are its obligations? Laura cannot say. She spends part of her days in Xochimilco, near by, teaching Indian children to say in English, "The cat is on the mat." When she appears in the classroom they crowd about her with smiles on their wise, innocent, clay-colored faces, crying, "Good morning, my titcher!" in immaculate voices, and they make of her desk a fresh garden of flowers every day.

During her leisure she goes to union meetings and listens to busy important voices quarreling over tactics, methods, internal politics. She visits the prisoners of her own political faith in their cells, where they entertain themselves with counting cockroaches, repenting of their indiscretions, composing their memoirs, writing out manifestoes and plans for their comrades who are still walking about free, hands in pockets, sniffing fresh air. Laura brings them food and cigarettes and a little money, and she brings messages disguised in equivocal phrases from the men outside who dare not set foot in the prison for fear of disappearing into the cells kept empty for them. If the prisoners confuse night and day, and complain, "Dear little Laura, time doesn't pass in this infernal hole, and I won't know when it is time to sleep unless I have a reminder," she brings them their favorite narcotics, and says in a tone that does not wound them with pity, "Tonight will really be night for you," and though her Spanish amuses them, they find her comforting, useful. If they lose patience and all faith, and curse the slowness of their friends in coming to their rescue with money and influence, they trust her not to repeat everything, and if she inquires, "Where do you think we can find money, or influence?" they are certain to answer, "Well, there is Braggioni, why doesn't he do something?"

She smuggles letters from headquarters to men hiding from firing squads in back streets in mildewed houses, where they sit in tumbled beds and talk bitterly

as if all Mexico were at their heels, when Laura knows
positively they might appear at the band concert in the
Alameda on Sunday morning, and no one would notice
them. But Braggioni says, "Let them sweat a little. The
next time they may be careful. It is very restful to have
them out of the way for a while." She is not afraid to
knock on any door in any street after midnight, and enter in the darkness, and say to one of these men who is
really in danger: "They will be looking for you—seriously—tomorrow morning after six. Here is some
money from Vicente. Go to Vera Cruz and wait."

She borrows money from the Roumanian agitator
to give to his bitter enemy the Polish agitator. The favor
of Braggioni is their disputed territory, and Braggioni
holds the balance nicely, for he can use them both. The
Polish agitator talks love to her over café tables, hoping
to exploit what he believes is her secret sentimental
preference for him, and he gives her misinformation
which he begs her to repeat as the solemn truth to certain persons. The Roumanian is more adroit. He is generous with his money in all good causes, and lies to her
with an air of ingenuous candor, as if he were her good
friend and confidant. She never repeats anything they
may say. Braggioni never asks questions. He has other
ways to discover all that he wishes to know about them.

Nobody touches her, but all praise her gray eyes,
and the soft, round underlip which promises gayety, yet
is always grave, nearly always firmly closed: and they
cannot understand why she is in Mexico. She walks
back and forth on her errands, with puzzled eyebrows,
carrying her little folder of drawings and music and
school papers. No dancer dances more beautifully than
Laura walks, and she inspires some amusing, unex-
pected ardors, which cause little gossip, because nothing comes of them. A young captain who had been a

soldier in Zapata's army attempted, during a horseback ride near Cuernavaca, to express his desire for her with the noble simplicity befitting a rude folk-hero: but gently, because he was gentle. This gentleness was his defeat, for when he alighted, and removed her foot from the stirrup, and essayed to draw her down into his arms, her horse, ordinarily a tame one, shied fiercely, reared and plunged away. The young hero's horse careered blindly after his stable-mate, and the hero did not return to the hotel until rather late that evening. At breakfast he came to her table in full charro dress, gray buckskin jacket and trousers with strings of silver buttons down the leg, and he was in a humorous, careless mood. "May I sit with you?" and "You are a wonderful rider. I was terrified that you might be thrown and dragged. I should never have forgiven myself. But I cannot admire you enough for your riding!"

"I learned to ride in Arizona," said Laura.

"If you will ride with me again this morning, I promise you a horse that will not shy with you," he said. But Laura remembered that she must return to Mexico City at noon.

Next morning the children made a celebration and spent their playtime writing on the chalkboard, "We lov ar ticher," and with tinted chalks they drew wreaths of flowers around the words. The young hero wrote her a letter: "I am a very foolish, wasteful, impulsive man. I should have first said I love you, and then you would not have run away. But you shall see me again." Laura thought, "I must send him a box of colored crayons," but she was trying to forgive herself for having spurred her horse at the wrong moment.

A brown, shock-haired youth came and stood in her patio one night and sang like a lost soul for two hours, but Laura could think of nothing to do about it.

The moonlight spread a wash of gauzy silver over the clear spaces of the garden, and the shadows were cobalt blue. The scarlet blossoms of the Judas tree were dull purple, and the names of the colors repeated themselves automatically in her mind, while she watched not the boy, but his shadow, fallen like a dark garment across the fountain rim, trailing in the water. Lupe came silently and whispered expert counsel in her ear: "If you will throw him one little flower, he will sing another song or two and go away." Laura threw the flower, and he sang a last song and went away with the flower tucked in the band of his hat. Lupe said, "He is one of the organizers of the Typographers Union, and before that he sold carridos in the Merced market, and before that, he came from Guanajuato, where I was born. I would not trust any man, but I trust least those from Guanajuato."

She did not tell Laura that he would be back again the next night, and the next, nor that he would follow her at a certain fixed distance around the Merced market, through the Zócolo, up Francisco I. Madero Avenue, and so along the Paseo de la Reforma to Chapultepec Park, and into the Philosopher's Footpath, still with that flower withering in his hat, and an indivisible attention in his eyes.

Now Laura is accustomed to him, it means nothing except that he is nineteen years old and is observing a convention with all propriety, as though it were founded on a law of nature, which in the end it might well prove to be. He is beginning to write poems which he prints on a wooden press, and he leaves them stuck like handbills in her door. She is pleasantly disturbed by the abstract, unhurried watchfulness of his black eyes which will in time turn easily towards another object. She tells herself that throwing the flower was a mistake, for she is twenty-two years old and knows better; but she refuses to regret it, and persuades herself that her negation of all external events as they occur is a sign that she is gradually perfecting herself in the stoicism she strives to cultivate against that disaster she fears, though she cannot name it.

She is not at home in the world. Every day she teaches children who remain strangers to her, though she loves their tender round hands and their charming opportunist savagery. She knocks at unfamiliar doors not knowing whether a friend or a stranger shall answer, and even if a known face emerges from the sour gloom of that unknown interior, still it is the face of a stranger. No matter what this stranger says to her, nor what her message to him, the very cells of her flesh reject knowledge and kinship in one monotonous word. No. No. No. She draws her strength from this one holy talismanic word which does not suffer her to be led into evil. Denying everything, she may walk anywhere in safety, she looks at everything without amazement.

No, repeats this firm unchanging voice of her blood; and she looks at Braggioni without amazement. He is a great man, he wishes to impress this simple girl who covers her great round breasts with thick dark cloth, and who hides long, invaluably beautiful legs under a heavy skirt. She is almost thin except for the incomprehensible fullness of her breasts, like a nursing mother's, and Braggioni, who considers himself a judge of women, speculates again on the puzzle of her notorious virginity, and takes the liberty of speech which she permits without a sign of modesty, indeed, without any sort of sign, which is disconcerting.

"You think you are so cold, *gringita!* Wait and see. You will surprise yourself some day! May I be there to advise you!" He stretches his eyelids at her, and his

ill-humored cat's eyes waver in a separate glance for the
two points of light marking the opposite ends of a
smoothly drawn path between the swollen curve of her
breasts. He is not put off by that blue serge, nor by her
resolutely fixed gaze. There is all the time in the world.
His cheeks are bellying with the wind of song. "O girl
with the dark eyes," he sings, and reconsiders. "But
yours are not dark. I can change all that. O girl with the
green eyes, you have stolen my heart away!" then his
mind wanders to the song, and Laura feels the weight
of his attention being shifted elsewhere. Singing thus,
he seems harmless, he is quite harmless, there is nothing to do but sit patiently and say "No," when the moment comes. She draws a full breath, and her mind
wanders also, but not far. She dares not wander too far.

Not for nothing has Braggioni taken pains to be a
good revolutionist and a professional lover of humanity.
He will never die of it. He has the malice, the cleverness, the wickedness, the sharpness of wit, the hardness of heart, stipulated for loving the world profitably.
He will never die of it. He will live to see himself kicked
out from his feeding trough by other hungry world-
saviors. Traditionally he must sing in spite of his life
which drives him to bloodshed, he tells Laura, for his
father was a Tuscany peasant who drifted to Yucatan
and married a Maya woman: a woman of race, an aristocrat. They gave him the love and knowledge of music,
thus: and under the rip of his thumbnail, the strings of
the instrument complain like exposed nerves.

Once he was called Delgadito by all the girls and
married women who ran after him; he was so scrawny
all his bones showed under his thin cotton clothing,
and he could squeeze his emptiness to the very backbone with his two hands. He was a poet and the revolution was only a dream then; too many women loved him

43

and sapped away his youth, and he could never find enough to eat anywhere, anywhere! Now he is a leader of men, crafty men who whisper in his ear, hungry men who wait for hours outside his office for a word with him, emaciated men with wild faces who waylay him at the street gate with a timid, "Comrade, let me tell you . . ." and they blow the foul breath from their empty stomachs in his face.

He is always sympathetic. He gives them hand-fuls of small coins from his own pocket, he promises them work, there will be demonstrations, they must join the unions and attend the meetings, above all they must be on the watch for spies. They are closer to him than his own brothers, without them he can do nothing—until tomorrow, comrade!

Until tomorrow, "They are stupid, they are lazy, they are treacherous, they would cut my throat for nothing," he says to Laura. He has good food and abundant drink, he hires an automobile and drives in the Paseo on Sunday morning, and enjoys plenty of sleep in a soft bed beside a wife who dares not disturb him; and he sits pampering his bones in easy billows of fat, singing to Laura, who knows and thinks these things about him. When he was fifteen, he tried to drown himself because he loved a girl, his first love, and she laughed at him. "A thousand women have paid for that," and his tight little mouth turns down at the corners. Now he perfumes his hair with Jockey Club, and confides to Laura: "One woman is really as good as another for me, in the dark. I prefer them all."

His wife organizes unions among the girls in the cigarette factories, and walks in picket lines, and even speaks at meetings in the evening. But she cannot be brought to acknowledge the benefits of true liberty. "I tell her I must have my freedom, net. She does not understand my point of view." Laura has heard this many times. Braggioni scratches the guitar and meditates. "She is an instinctively virtuous woman, pure gold, no doubt of that. If she were not, I should lock her up, and she knows it."

His wife, who works so hard for the good of the factory girls, employs part of her leisure lying on the floor weeping because there are so many women in the world, and only one husband for her, and she never knows where or when to look for him. He told her: "Unless you can learn to cry when I am not here, I must go away for good." That day he went away and took a room at the Hotel Madrid.

It is this month of separation for the sake of higher principles that has been spoiled not only for Mrs. Braggioni, whose sense of reality is beyond criticism, but also for Laura, who feels herself bogged in a nightmare. Tonight Laura envies Mrs. Braggioni, who is alone, and free to weep as much as she pleases about a concrete wrong. Laura has just come from a visit to the prison, and she is waiting for tomorrow with a bitter anxiety as if tomorrow may not come, but time may be caught immovably in this hour, with herself transfixed, Braggioni singing on forever, and Eugenio's body not yet discovered by the guard.

Braggioni says: "Are you going to sleep?" Almost before she can shake her head, he begins telling her about the May-day disturbances coming on in Morelia, for the Catholics hold a festival in honor of the Blessed Virgin, and the Socialists celebrate their martyrs on that day. "There will be two independent processions, starting from either end of town, and they will march until they meet, and the rest depends . . ." He asks her to oil and load his pistols. Standing up, he unbuckles his ammunition belt, and spreads it laden across her knees. Laura sits with the shells slipping through the cleaning cloth dipped in oil, and he says again he cannot understand why she works so hard for the revolutionary idea unless she loves some man who is in it. "Are you not in love with someone?" "No," says Laura. "And no one is in love with you?" "No." "Then it is your own fault. No woman need go begging. Why, what is the matter with you? The legless beggar woman in the Alameda has a perfectly faithful lover. Did you know that?"

Laura peers down the pistol barrel and says nothing, but a long, slow faintness rises and subsides in her; Braggioni curves his swollen fingers around the throat of the guitar and softly smothers the music out of it, and when she hears him again he seems to have forgotten her, and is speaking in the hypnotic voice he uses when talking in small rooms to a listening, close-gathered crowd. Some day this world, now seemingly so composed and eternal, to the edges of every sea shall be merely a tangle of gaping trenches, of crashing walls and broken bodies. Everything must be torn from its accustomed place where it has rotted for centuries, hurled skyward and distributed, cast down again clean as rain, without separate identity. Nothing shall survive that the stiffened hands of poverty have created for the rich and no one shall be left alive except the elect spirits destined to procreate a new world cleansed of cruelty and injustice, ruled by benevolent anarchy: "Pistols are good, I love them, cannon are even better, but in the end I pin my faith to good dynamite," he concludes, and strokes the pistol lying in her hands. "Once I dreamed of destroying this city, in case it offered resistance to General Ortíz, but it fell into his hands like an overripe pear."

He is made restless by his own words, rises and

stands waiting. Laura holds up the belt to him: "Put that on, and go kill somebody in Morelia, and you will be happier," she says softly. The presence of death in the room makes her bold. "Today, I found Eugenio going into a stupor. He refused to allow me to call the prison doctor. He had taken all the tablets I brought him yesterday. He said he took them because he was bored."

"He is a fool, and his death is his own business," says Braggioni, fastening his belt carefully.

"I told him if he had waited only a little while longer, you would have got him set free," says Laura. "He said he did not want to wait."

"He is a fool and we are well rid of him," says Braggioni, reaching for his hat.

He goes away. Laura knows his mood has changed, she will not see him any more for a while. He will send word when he needs her to go on errands into strange streets, to speak to the strange faces that will appear, like clay masks with the power of human speech, to mutter their thanks to Braggioni for his help. Now she is free, and she thinks, I must run while there is time. But she does not go.

Braggioni enters his own house where for a month his wife spent many hours every night weeping and tangling her hair upon her pillow. She is weeping now, and she weeps more at the sight of him, the cause of all her sorrows. He looks about the room. Nothing is changed, the smells are good and familiar, he is well acquainted with the woman who comes toward him with no reproach except grief on her face. He says to her tenderly: "You are so good, please don't cry any more, you dear good creature." She says, "Are you tired, my angel? Sit here and I will wash your feet." She brings a bowl of water, and kneeling, unlaces his shoes, and when from her knees she raises her sad eyes under her blackened lids, he is sorry for everything, and bursts into tears. "Ah, yes, I am hungry, I am tired, let us eat something together," he says, between sobs. His wife leans her head on his arm and says, "Forgive me!" and this time he is refreshed by the solemn, endless rain of her tears.

Laura takes off her serge dress and puts on a white linen nightgown and goes to bed. She turns her head a little to one side, and lying still, reminds herself that it is time to sleep. Numbers tick in her brain like little clocks, soundless doors close of themselves around her. If you would sleep, you must not remember anything, the children will say tomorrow, good morning, my teacher, the poor prisoners who come every day bringing flowers to their jailor, 1–2–3–4–5—it is monstrous to confuse love with revolution, night with day, life with death—ah, Eugenio!

The tolling of the midnight bell is a signal, but what does it mean? Get up, Laura, and follow me: come out of your sleep, out of your bed, out of this strange house. What are you doing in this house? Without a word, without fear she rose and reached for Eugenio's hand, but he eluded her with a sharp, sly smile and drifted away. This is not all, you shall see—Murderer, he said, follow me, I will show you a new country, but it is far away and we must hurry. No, said Laura, not unless you take my hand, no; and she clung first to the stair rail, and then to the topmost branch of the Judas tree that bent down slowly and set her upon the earth, and then to the rocky ledge of a cliff, and then to the jagged wave of a sea that was not water but a desert of crumbling stone. Where are you taking me, she asked in wonder but without fear. To death, and it is a long way off, and we must hurry, said Eugenio. No, said

Laura, not unless you take my hand. Then eat these
flowers, poor prisoner, said Eugenio in a voice of pity,
take and eat: and from the Judas tree he stripped the
warm bleeding flowers, and held them to her lips. She
saw that his hand was fleshless, a cluster of small white
petrified branches, and his eye sockets were without
light, but she ate the flowers greedily for they satisfied
both hunger and thirst. Murderer! said Eugenio, and
Cannibal! This is my body and my blood. Laura cried
No! and at the sound of her own voice, she awoke trembling, and was afraid to sleep again.

Background
to the Story

Why [I] Selected "Flowering Judas"

"Flowering Judas" was written between seven o'clock and midnight of a very cold December, 1929, in Brooklyn. The experiences from which it was made occurred several years before, in Mexico, just after the Obregón revolution.

All the characters and episodes are based on real persons and events, but naturally, as my memory worked upon them and time passed, all assumed different shapes and colors, formed gradually around a central idea, that of self-delusion, the order and meaning of the episodes changed, and became in a word fiction.

The idea first came to me one evening when going to visit the girl I call Laura in the story, I passed the open window of her living room on my way to the door, through the small patio which is one of the scenes in the story. I had a brief glimpse of her sitting with an open book in her lap, but not reading, with a fixed look of pained melancholy and confusion in her face. The fat man I called Braggioni was playing the guitar and singing to her.

In that glimpse, no more than a flash, I thought I understood, or perceived, for the first time, the desperate complications of her mind and feelings, and I knew a story; perhaps not her true story, not even the real story of the whole situation, but all the same a story that seemed symbolic truth to me. If I had not seen her face at that very moment, I should never have written just this story because I should not have known it to write.

The editor has asked for my favorite story. I have no

From *This is My Best*, Whit Burnett, ed. (New York: The Dial Press, 1942), 539–540.

53

favorites though there is perhaps one, a short novel, for which now and then I do feel a preference, for extremely personal reasons. I offer this story which falls within the stipulated length because it comes very near to being what I meant for it to be, and I suppose an author's choice of his own work must always be decided by such private knowledge of the margin between intention and the accomplished fact.

Boulder, Colo.
July 13, 1942

Why I Write About Mexico

*(a Letter to the Editor
of* The Century*)*

I write about Mexico because that is my familiar country. I was born near San Antonio, Texas. My father lived part of his youth in Mexico, and told me enchanting stories of his life there; therefore the land did not seem strange to me even at my first sight of it. During the Madero revolution I watched a street battle between Maderistas and Federal troops from the window of a cathedral; a grape-vine heavy with tiny black grapes formed a screen, and a very old Indian woman stood near me, perfectly silent, holding my sleeve. Later she said to me, when the dead were being piled for burning in the public square, "It is all a great trouble now, but it is for the sake of happiness to come." She crossed herself, and I mistook her meaning.

"In heaven?" I asked. Her scorn was splendid.

"No, on earth. Happiness for men, not for angels!"

She seemed to me then to have caught the whole meaning of revolution, and to have said it in a phrase. From that day I watched Mexico, and all the apparently unrelated events that grew out of that first struggle never seemed false or alien or aimless to me. A straight, undeviating purpose guided the working of the plan. And it permitted many fine things to grow out of the national soil, only faintly surmised during the last two or three centuries even by the Mexicans themselves. It was as if an old field had been watered, and all the long-buried seeds flourished.

About three years ago I returned to Mexico, after a long absence, to study the renascence of Mexican art—a veritable

From *The Collected Essays and Occasional Writings of Katherine Anne Porter* (New York: Delacorte Press, 1970).

rebirth, very conscious, very powerful, of a deeply racial and personal art. I was not won to it by any artificial influence; I recognized it at once as something very natural and acceptable, a feeling for art consanguine with my own, unfolding in a revolution which returned to find its freedoms in profound and honorable sources. It would be difficult to explain in a very few words how the Mexicans have enriched their national life through the medium of their native arts. It is in everything they do and are. I cannot say, "I gathered material" for it; there was nothing so mechanical as that, but the process of absorption went on almost unconsciously, and my impressions remain not merely as of places visited and people known, but as of a moving experience in my own life that is now a part of me.

My stories are fragments, each one touching some phase of a versatile national temperament, which is a complication of simplicities: but I like best the quality of aesthetic magnificence, and, above all, the passion for individual expression without hypocrisy, which is the true genius of the race.

I have been accused by Americans of a taste for the exotic, for foreign flavors. Maybe so, for New York is the most foreign place I know, and I like it very much. But in my childhood I knew the French-Spanish people in New Orleans and the strange "Cajans" in small Louisiana towns, with their curious songs and customs and blurred patois; the German colonists in Texas and the Mexicans of the San Antonio country, until it seemed to me that all my life I had lived among people who spoke broken, laboring tongues, who put on with terrible difficulty, yet with such good faith, the ways of the dominant race about them. This is true here in New York also, I know: but I have never thought of these people as any other than American. Literally speaking, I have never been out of America; but my America has been a borderland of strange tongues and commingled races, and if they are not American, I am fearfully mistaken. The artist can do no more than deal with familiar and beloved things, from which he could not, and, above all, would not escape. So I claim that I write of things native to me, that part of America to which I belong by birth and association and temperament, which is as much the province of our native literature as Chicago or New York or San Francisco. All the things I write of I have first known, and they are real to me.

The Mexican Trinity

(*Report from Mexico City,*
July, 1921)

Uneasiness grows here daily. We are having sudden deportations of foreign agitators, street riots and parades of workers carrying red flags. Plots thicken, thin, disintegrate in the space of thirty-six hours. A general was executed today for counterrevolutionary activities. There is fevered discussion in the newspapers as to the best means of stamping out Bolshevism, which is the inclusive term for all forms of radical work. Battles occur almost daily between Catholics and Socialists in many parts of the Republic: Morelia, Yucatán, Campeche, Jalisco. In brief, a clamor of petty dissension almost drowns the complicated debate between Mexico and the United States.

It is fascinating to watch, but singularly difficult to record because events overlap, and the news of today may be stale before it reaches the border. It is impossible to write fully of the situation unless one belongs to that choice company of folk who can learn all about peoples and countries in a couple of weeks. We have had a constant procession of these strange people: they come dashing in, gather endless notes and dash out again and three weeks later their expert, definitive opinions are published. Marvelous! I have been here for seven months, and for quite six of these I have not been sure of what the excitement is all about. Indeed, I am not yet able to say whether my accumulated impression of Mexico is justly proportioned; or that if I write with profound conviction of what is going on I shall not be making a profoundly comical mistake. The true story of a people is not to be had exclusively

From *The Collected Essays and Occasional Writings of Katherine Anne Porter* (New York: Delacorte Press, 1970).

57

from official documents, or from guarded talks with diplomats. Nor is it to be gathered entirely from the people themselves. The life of a great nation is too widely scattered and complex and vast; too many opposing forces are at work, each with its own intensity of self seeking.

Has any other country besides Mexico so many types of enemy within the gates? Here they are both foreign and native, hostile to each other by tradition, but mingling their ambitions in a common cause. The Mexican capitalist joins forces with the American against his revolutionary fellow-countryman. The Catholic Church enlists the help of Protestant strangers in the subjugation of the Indian, clamoring for his land. Reactionary Mexicans work faithfully with reactionary foreigners to achieve their ends by devious means. The Spanish, a scourge of Mexico, have plans of their own and are no better loved than they ever were. The British, Americans and French seek political and financial power, oil and mines; a splendid horde of invaders, they are distrustful of each other, but unable to disentangle their interests. Then there are the native bourgeoisie, much resembling the bourgeoisie elsewhere, who are opposed to all idea of revolution. "We want peace, and more business," they chant uniformly, but how these blessings are to be obtained they do not know. "More business, and no Bolshevism!" is their cry, and they are ready to support any man or group of men who can give them what they want. The professional politicians of Mexico likewise bear a strong family likeness to gentlemen engaged in this line of business in other parts of the world. Some of them have their prejudices; it may be against the Americans, or against the Church, or against the radicals, or against the other local political party, but whatever their prejudices may be they are pathetically unanimous in their belief that big business will save the country.

The extreme radical group includes a number of idealists, somewhat tragic figures these, for their cause is so hopeless. They are nationalists of a fanatical type, recalling the early Sinn Feiners. They are furious and emotional and reasonless and determined. They want, God pity them, a free Mexico at once. Any conservative newspaper editor will tell you what a hindrance they are to the "best minds" who are now trying to make the going easy for big business. If a reasonable government is to get any work done, such misguided enthusiasts can not be disposed of too quickly. A few cooler revolutionists have been working toward civilized alleviations of present distresses pending the coming of the perfect State. Such harmless institutions as free schools for the workers, including a course in social science, have been set going. Clinics, dispensaries, birth-control information for the appallingly fertile Mexican woman, playgrounds for children—it sounds almost like the routine program of any East Side social-service worker. But here in Mexico such things have become dangerous, bolshevistic. Among the revolutionists, the Communists have been a wildly disturbing element. This cult was composed mostly of discontented foreigners, lacking even the rudiments of the Russian theory, with not a working revolutionist among them. The Mexicans, when they are not good party-revolutionists, are simple syndicalists of an extreme type. By party-revolutionists I mean the followers of some leader who is not an adherent of any particular revolutionary formula, but who is bent on putting down whatever government happens to be in power and establishing his own, based on a purely nationalistic ideal of reform.

The present government of Mexico is made up of certain intensely radical people, combined with a cast-iron reactionary group which was added during the early days of the administration. In the Cabinet at the extreme left wing is Calles, the most radical public official in Mexico today, modified by de la Huerta at his elbow. At the extreme right wing is Alberto Pani, Minister of Foreign Relations, and Capmany, Minister of Labor. The other members are political gradations of these four minds. The pull-and-haul is intense and never ceases. Such a coalition government for Mexico is a great idea, and the theory is not unfamiliar to American minds: that all classes have the right to equal representation in the government. But it will not work. Quite naturally, all that any group of politicians wants is their own way in everything. They will fight to the last ditch to get it; coalition be hanged!

The revolution has not yet entered into the souls of the Mexican people. There can be no doubt of that. What is going on here is not the resistless upheaval of a great mass leavened by teaching and thinking and suffering. The Russian writers made the Russian Revolution, I verily believe, through a period of seventy-five years' preoccupation with the wrongs of the peasant, and the cruelties of life under the heel of the Tsar. Here in Mexico there is no conscience crying through the literature of the country. A small group of intellectuals still writes about romance and the stars, and roses and the shadowy eyes of ladies, touching no sorrow of the human heart other than the pain of unrequited love.

But then, the Indians cannot read. What good would a literature of revolt do them? Yet they are the very life of the country, this inert and slow-breathing mass, these lost people who move in the oblivion of sleepwalkers under their incredible burdens; these silent and reproachful figures in rags, bowed face to face with the earth; it is these who bind together all the accumulated and hostile elements of Mexican life. Leagued against the Indian are four centuries of servitude, the incoming foreigner who will take the last hectare of his land, and his own church that stands with the foreigners.

It is generally understood in Mexico that one of the conditions of recognition by the United States is that all radicals holding office in the Cabinet and in the lesser departments of government must go. That is what must be done if Mexico desires peace with the United States. This means, certainly, the dismissal of everyone who is doing constructive work in lines that ought to be far removed from the field of politics, such as education and welfare work among the Indians.

Everybody here theorizes endlessly. Each individual member of the smallest subdivision of the great triumvirate, Land, Oil, and the Church, has his own pet theory, fitting his prophecy to his desire. Everybody is in the confidence of somebody else who knows everything long before it happens. In this way one hears of revolutions to be started tomorrow or the next day or the day after that; but though the surface shifts and changes, one can readily deduce for oneself that one static combination remains, Land, Oil, and the Church. In principle these three are one. They do not take part in these petty national dissensions. Their battleground is the world. If the oil companies are to get oil, they need land. If the Church is to have wealth, it needs land. The partition of land in Mexico, therefore, menaces not only the *haciendados* (individual landholders), but foreign investors and the very foundations of the Church. Already, under the land-reform laws of Juárez, the Church cannot hold land; it evades this decree, however, by holding property in guardianship, but even this title will be destroyed by repartition.

The recent encounters between Catholics and Socialists in different parts of Mexico have been followed by a spectacular activity on the part of the Catholic clergy. They are pulling their old familiar wires, and all the bedraggled puppets are dancing with a great clatter. The clever ones indulge in skillful moves in the political game, and there are street brawls for the hot-heads. For the peons there is always the moldy, infallible device; a Virgin—this time of Guadalupe—has been seen to move, to shine miraculously in a darkened room! A poor woman in Puebla was favored by Almighty God with the sight of this miracle, just at the moment of the Church's greatest political uncertainty; and now this miraculous image is to be brought here to Mexico City. The priests are insisting on a severe investigation to be carried on by themselves, and the statue is to be placed in an *oratorio,* where it will be living proof to the faithful that the great patroness of Mexico has set her face against reform.

The peons are further assured by the priests that to accept the land given to them by the reform laws is to be guilty of simple stealing, and everyone taking such land will be excluded from holy communion—a very effective threat. The agents who come to survey the land for the purposes of partition are attacked by the very peons they have come to benefit. Priests who warn their congregations against the new land-laws have been arrested and imprisoned, and now and then a stick of dynamite has been hurled at a bishop's palace by a radical hot-head. But these things do not touch the mighty power of the Church, solidly entrenched as it is in its growing strength, and playing the intricate game of international politics with gusto and skill.

So far, I have not talked with a single member of the American colony here who does not eagerly watch for the show to begin. They want American troops in here, and want them quickly—they are apprehensive that the soldiers will not arrive soon enough, and that they will be left to the mercy of the Mexicans for several weeks, maybe. It is strange talk one hears. It is indulged in freely over café tables and on street-corners, at teas and at dances.

61

Meanwhile international finance goes on its own appointed way. The plans that were drawn up more than a year ago by certain individuals who manage these things in the United States, are going forward nicely, and are being hampered no more than normally by upstarts who have plans of their own. Inevitably certain things will have to be done when the time comes, with only a few necessary deviations due to the workings of the "imponderables." The whole program has been carefully worked out by Oil, Land, and the Church, the powers that hold this country securely in their grip.

Katherine Anne Porter: An Interview

The Victorian house in which Katherine Anne Porter lives is nar row and white, reached by an iron-railed stairway curving up from the shady brick-walked Georgetown street. The parlor to which a maid admits the caller is an elegant mélange of several aspects of the past, both American and European. High-ceilinged, dim and cool after the midsummer glare, the room is dominated by a bottle-green settee from the period of Napoleon III. Outside the alcove of windows there is a rustle of wind through ginkgo trees, then a hush.

Finally, a voice in the upper hallway: its tone that of someone talking to a bird, or coquetting with an old beau—light and feathery, with a slight flutter. A few moments later, moving as lightly as her voice, Miss Porter hurries through the wide doorway, unexpectedly modern in a soft green suit of woven Italian silk. Small and elegant, she explains her tardiness, relates an anecdote of the morning's mail, offers a minted ice tea, and speculates aloud on where we might best conduct our conversation.

She decides on the dining room, a quiet, austere place overlooking the small enclosed garden. Here the aspect is a different one. "I want to live in a world capital or the howling wilderness," she said once, and did. The drawing room was filled with pieces that had once been part of the house on rue Notre-Dame des Champs; this one is bright with Mexican folk art—whistles and toy animals collected during a recent tour for the Department of State—against simpler, heavier pieces of furniture. The round table at which we sit is of Vermont marble, mottled and colored like milk glass, on a wrought-iron base of her own design. There is a sixteenth-century cupboard from Avila, and a refectory table of the early Renaissance from a convent in Fiesole. Here we settle the tape recorder, under an image of the great god Horus.

We try to make a beginning. She is an experienced lecturer, familiar with microphone and tape recorder, but now she is to talk about herself as well as her work,

From *Writers at Work: The Paris Review Interviews, Second Series* (New York: Viking Press, 1963).

the link between, and the inexorable winding of the tape from one spool to the other acts almost as a hypnotic. Finally we turn it off and talk for a while of other things, more frivolous and more autobiographical, hoping to surprise an easier revelation.

INTERVIEWER: You were saying that you had never intended to make a career of writing.

PORTER: I've never made a career of anything, you know, not even of writing. I started out with nothing in the world but a kind of passion, a driving desire. I don't know where it came from, and I don't know why—or why I have been so stubborn about it that nothing could deflect me. But this thing between me and my writing is the strongest bond I have ever had— stronger than any bond or any engagement with any human being or with any other work I've ever done. I really started writing when I was six or seven years old. But I had such a multiplicity of half-talents, too: I wanted to dance, I wanted to play the piano, I sang, I drew. It wasn't really dabbling—I was investigating everything, experimenting in everything. And then, for one thing, there weren't very many amusements in those days. If you wanted music, you had to play the piano and sing yourself. Oh, we saw all the great things that came during the season, but after all, there would only be a dozen or so of those occasions a year. The rest of the time we depended upon our own resources: our own music and books. All the old houses that I knew when I was a child were full of books, bought generation after generation by members of the family. Everyone was literate as a matter of course. Nobody told you to read this or not to read that. It was there to read, and we read.

INTERVIEWER: Which books influenced you most?

PORTER: That's hard to say, because I grew up in a sort of mélange. I was reading Shakespeare's sonnets when I was thirteen years old, and I'm perfectly certain that they made the most profound impression upon me of anything I ever read. For a time I knew the whole sequence by heart; now I can only remember two or three of them. That was the turning point of my life, when I read the Shakespeare sonnets, and then all at one blow, all of Dante—in that great big book illustrated by Gustave Doré. The plays I saw on the stage, but I don't remember reading them with any interest at all. Oh, and I read all kinds of poetry—Homer, Ronsard, all the old French poets in translation. We also had a very good library of—well, you might say secular philosophers. I was incredibly influenced by Montaigne when I was very young. And one day when I was about fourteen, my father led me up to a great big line of books and said, "Why don't you read this? It'll knock some of the nonsense out of you!" It happened to be the entire set of Voltaire's philosophical dictionary with notes by Smollett. And I plowed through it; it took me about five years.

And of course we read all the eighteenth-century novelists, though Jane Austen, like Turgenev, didn't really engage me until I was quite mature. I read them both when I was very young, but I was grown up before I really took them in. And I discovered for myself *Wuthering Heights;* I think I read that book every year of my life for fifteen years. I simply adored it. Henry James and Thomas Hardy were really my introduction to modern literature; Grandmother didn't much approve of it. She thought Dickens might do, but she was a little against Mr. Thackeray; she thought he was too trivial. So that was as far as I got into the modern world until I left home!

INTERVIEWER: Don't you think this background—the comparative isolation of Southern rural life, and the atmosphere of literary interest—helped to shape you as a writer?

PORTER: I think it's something in the blood. We've always had great letter writers, readers, great storytellers in our family. I've listened all my life to articulate people. They were all great storytellers, and every story had shape and meaning and point.

INTERVIEWER: Were any of them known as writers?

PORTER: Well, there was my sixth or seventh cousin once removed, poor William Sidney. O. Henry, you know. He was my father's second cousin—I don't know what that makes him to me. And he was more known in the family for being a bank robber. He worked in a bank, you know, and he just didn't seem to find a talent for making money; no Porter ever did.

But he had a wife who was dying of TB and he couldn't keep up with the doctor's bills. So he took a pitiful little sum—oh, about three hundred and fifty dollars—and ran away when he was accused. But he came back, because his wife was dying, and went to prison. And there was Horace Porter, who spent his whole eight years as ambassador to France looking for the bones of John Paul Jones. And when he found them, and brought them back, he wrote a book about them.

INTERVIEWER: It seems to me that your work is pervaded by a sense of history. Is that part of the family legacy?

PORTER: We were brought up with a sense of our own history, you know. My mother's family came to this country in 1648 and went to the John Randolph territory of Virginia. And one of my great great grandfathers was Jonathan Boone, the brother of Daniel. On my father's side I'm descended from Colonel Andrew Porter, whose father came to Montgomery County, Pennsylvania, in 1720. He was one of the circle of George Washington during the Revolution, a friend of Lafayette, and one of the founders of the Society of the Cincinnati—oh, he really took it seriously!—and when he died in 1809—well, just a few years before that he was offered the post of Secretary of War, but he declined. We were never very ambitious people. We never had a President, though we had two governors and some in the Army and the Navy. I suppose we did have a desire to excel but not to push our way to higher places. We thought we'd *already* arrived!

INTERVIEWER: The "we" of family is very strong, isn't it? I remember that you once wrote of the ties of blood as the "absolute point of all departure and return." And the central character in many of your stories is defined, is defining herself often, in relation to a family organization. Even the measure of time is human—expressed in terms of the very old and the very young, and how much of human experience they have absorbed.

PORTER: Yes, but it wasn't a conscious made-up affair, you know. In those days you belonged together, you lived together, because you were a family. The head of our house was a grandmother, an old matriarch, you know, and a really lovely and beautiful woman, a good soul, and so she didn't do us any harm. But the point is that we did live like that, with Grand-mother's friends, all reverend old gentlemen with frock coats, and old ladies with jet breastplates. Then there were the younger people, the beautiful girls and the handsome young boys, who were all ahead of me; when I was a little girl, eight or nine years old, they were eighteen to twenty-two, and they represented all glamour, all beauty, all joy and freedom to me. Then there was my own age, and then there were the babies. And the servants, the Negroes. We simply lived that way; to have four generations in one house, under one roof, there was nothing unusual about that. That was just my experience, and this is just the way I've reacted to it. Many other people didn't react, who were brought up in very much the same way.

I remember when I was very young, my older sister wanted to buy some old furniture. It was in Louisiana, and she had just been married. And I went with her to a wonderful old house in the country where we'd been told there was a very old gentleman who probably had some things to sell. His wife had died, and he was living there alone. So we went to this lovely old house, and sure enough, there was this lonely beau-tiful old man, eighty-seven or -eight, surrounded by devoted Negro servants. But his wife was dead and his children were married and gone. He said, yes, he had a few things he wanted to sell. So he showed us through the house. And finally he opened a door, and showed us a bedroom with a beautiful four-poster bed, with a wonderful satin coverlet: the most wonder-ful, classical-looking bed you ever saw. And my sister said, "Oh, that's what I want!" And he said, "Oh, madame, that is my marriage bed. That is the bed that my wife brought with her as a bride. We slept together in that bed for nearly sixty years. All our children were born there. Oh," he said, "I shall die in that bed, and then they can dispose of it as they like."

I remember that I felt a little suffocated and frightened. I felt a little trapped. But why? Only because I understood that. I was brought up in that. And I was at the age of rebellion then, and it really scared me. But I look back on it now and think how perfectly wonderful, what a tremendously beautiful life it was. Everything in it had meaning.

INTERVIEWER: But it seems to me that your work suggests someone who was searching for new—perhaps broader—

meanings . . . that while you've retained the South of your childhood as a point of reference, you've ranged far from that environment itself. You seem to have felt little of the peculiarly Southern preoccupation with racial guilt and the death of the old agrarian life.

PORTER: I'm a Southerner by tradition and inheritance, and I have a very profound feeling for the South. And, of course, I belong to the guilt-ridden white-pillar crowd myself, but it just didn't rub off on me. Maybe I'm just not Jewish enough, or Puritan enough, to feel that the sins of the father are visited on the third and fourth generations. Or maybe it's because of my European influences—in Texas and Louisiana. The European didn't have slaves themselves as late as my family did, but they *still* thought slavery was quite natural. . . . But, you know, I was always restless, always a roving spirit. When I was a little child I was always running away. I never got very far, but they were always having to come and fetch me. Once when I was about six, my father came to get me somewhere I'd gone, and he told me later he'd asked me, "Why are you so restless? Why can't you stay here with us?" and I said to him, "I want to go and see the world. I want to know the world like the palm of my hand."

INTERVIEWER: And at sixteen you made it final.

PORTER: At sixteen I ran away from New Orleans and got married. And at twenty-one I bolted again, went to Chicago, got a newspaper job, and went into the movies.

INTERVIEWER: The movies?

PORTER: The newspaper sent me over to the old S. and A. movie studio to do a story. But I got into the wrong line, and then was too timid to get out. "Right over this way, Little Boy Blue," the man said, and I found myself in a courtroom scene with Francis X. Bushman. I was horrified by what had happened to me, but they paid me five dollars for that first day's work, so I stayed on. It was about a week before I remembered what I had been sent to do; and when I went back to the newspaper they gave me eighteen dollars for my week's non-work and fired me!

I stayed on for six months—I finally got to nearly ten

dollars a day—until one day they came in and said, "We're moving to the coast." "Well, I'm not," I said. "Don't you want to be a movie actress?" "Oh, no!" I said. "Well, be a fool!" they said, and they left. That was 1914 and World War I had broken out, so in September I went home.

INTERVIEWER: And then?

PORTER: Oh, I sang old Scottish ballads in costume—I made it myself—all around Texas and Louisiana. And then I was supposed to have TB, and spent about six weeks in a sanitarium. It was just bronchitis, but I was in Denver, so I got a newspaper job.

INTERVIEWER: I remember that you once warned me to avoid that at all costs—to get a job "hashing" in a restaurant in preference.

PORTER: Anything, anything at all. I did it for a year and that is what confirmed to me that it wasn't doing me any good. After that I always took little dull jobs that didn't take my mind and wouldn't take all of my time, and that, on the other hand, paid me just enough to subsist. I think I've only spent about ten per cent of my energies on writing. The other ninety per cent went to keeping my head above water.

And I think that's all wrong. Even Saint Teresa said, "I can pray better when I'm comfortable," and she refused to wear her haircloth shirt or starve herself. I don't think living in cellars and starving is any better for an artist than it is for anybody else; the only thing is that sometimes the artist has to take it, because it is the only possible way of salvation, if you'll forgive that old-fashioned word. So I took it rather instinctively. I was inexperienced in the world, and likewise I hadn't been trained to do anything, you know, so I took all kinds of laborious jobs. But, you know, I think I could probably have written better if I'd been a little more comfortable.

INTERVIEWER: Then you were writing all this time?

PORTER: All this time I was writing, writing no matter what else I was doing; no matter what I *thought* I was doing, in fact. I was living almost as instinctively as a little animal, but I realize now that all that time a part of me was getting ready to be an artist. That my mind was working even when I didn't know it, and didn't care if it was working or not. It is my firm belief that all our lives we are preparing to be somebody or something, even if we don't do it consciously. And the time comes one morning when you wake up and find that you have become irrevocably what you were preparing all this time to be. Lord, that could be a sticky moment, if you had been doing the wrong things, something against your grain. And, mind you, I know that can happen. I have no patience with this dreadful idea that whatever you have in you has to come out, that you can't suppress true talent. People *can* be destroyed; they can be bent, distorted, and completely crippled. To say that you can't destroy yourself is just as foolish as to say of a young man killed in war at twenty-one or twenty-two that that was his fate, that he wasn't going to have anything anyhow.

I have a very firm belief that the life of no man can be explained in terms of his experiences, of what has happened to him, because in spite of all the poetry, all the philosophy to the contrary, we are not really masters of our fate. We don't really direct our lives unaided and unobstructed. Our being is subject to all the chances of life. There are so many things we are capable of, that we could be or do. The potentialities are so great that we never, any of us, are more than one-fourth fulfilled. Except that there may be one powerful motivating force that simply carries you along, and I think that was true of me. . . . When I was a very little girl I wrote a letter to my sister saying I wanted glory. I don't know quite what I meant by that now, but it was something different from fame or success or wealth. I know that I wanted to be a good writer, a good artist.

INTERVIEWER: But weren't there certain specific events that crystallized that desire for you—something comparable to the experience of Miranda in *Pale Horse, Pale Rider*?

PORTER: Yes, that was the plague of influenza, at the end of the First World War, in which I almost died. It just simply divided my life, cut across it like that. So that everything before that was just getting ready, and after that I was in some strange way altered, ready. It took me a long time to go out and live in the world again. I was really "alienated," in the pure sense. It was, I think, the fact that I really had participated in death, that I knew what death was, and had almost experienced it. I had what the Christians call the "beatific vision," and the Greeks called the "happy day," the happy vision just before death. Now if you have had that, and survived it, come back from it, you are no longer like other people, and there's no use deceiving yourself that you are. But you see, I did: I made the mistake of thinking I was quite like anybody else, of trying to live like other people. It took me a long time to realize that that simply wasn't true, that I had my own needs and that I had to live like me.

INTERVIEWER: And that freed you?

PORTER: I just got up and bolted. I went running off on that wild escapade to Mexico, where I attended, you might say, and assisted at, in my own modest way, a revolution.

INTERVIEWER: That was the Obregón Revolution in 1921?

PORTER: Yes—though actually I went to Mexico to study the Aztec and Mayan art designs. I had been in New York, and was getting ready to go to Europe. Now, New York was full of Mexican artists at that time, all talking about the renaissance, as they called it, in Mexico. And they said, "Don't go to Europe, go to Mexico. That's where the exciting things are going to happen." And they were right! I ran smack into the Obregón Revolution, and had, in the midst of it, the most marvelous, natural, spontaneous experience of my life. It was a terribly exciting time. It was alive, but death was in it. But nobody seemed to think of that: life was in it, too.

INTERVIEWER: What do you think are the best conditions for a writer, then? Something like your Mexican experience, or—

PORTER: Oh, I can't say what they are. It would be such an individual matter. Everyone needs something different. . . . But what I find most dreadful among the young artists is this tendency toward middle-classness—this idea that they have to get married and have lots of children and live just like everybody else, you know? Now, I am all for human life, and I am all for marriage and children and all that sort of thing, but quite often you can't have that and do what you were supposed to do, too. Art is a vocation, as much as anything in this world. For the real artist, it is the most natural thing in the world, not as necessary as air and water, perhaps, but as food and water.

71

But we really do lead almost a monastic life, you know; to follow it you very often have to give up something.

INTERVIEWER: But for the unproven artist that is a very great act of faith.

PORTER: It *is* an act of faith. But one of the marks of a gift is to have the courage of it. If they haven't got the courage, it's just too bad. They'll fail, just as people with lack of courage in other vocations and walks of life fail. Courage is the first essential.

INTERVIEWER: Is choosing a pattern of life compatible with the vocation?

PORTER: The thing is not to follow a pattern. Follow your own pattern of feeling and thought. The thing is, to accept your own life and not try to live someone else's life. Look, the thumbprint is not like any other, and the thumbprint is what you must go by.

INTERVIEWER: In the current vernacular then, you think it's necessary for an artist to be a "loner"—not to belong to any literary movement?

PORTER: I've never belonged to any group or huddle of any kind. You cannot be an artist and work collectively. Even the fact that I went to Mexico when everybody else was going to Europe—I went to Mexico because I felt I had business there. And there I found friends and ideas that were sympathetic to me. That was my entire milieu. I don't think anyone even knew I was a writer. I didn't show my work to anybody or talk about it, because—well, no one was particularly interested in that. It was a time of revolution, and I was running with almost pure revolutionaries!

INTERVIEWER: And you think that was a more wholesome environment for a writer than, say, the milieu of the expatriated artist in Europe at the same time?

PORTER: Well, I know it was good for me. I would have been completely smothered—completely disgusted and revolted—by the goings-on in Europe. Even now when I think of the twenties and the legend that has grown up about them, I think it was a horrible time: shallow and trivial and silly. The remarkable thing is that anybody survived in such an atmosphere—in a place where they could call F. Scott Fitzgerald a great writer!

INTERVIEWER: You don't agree?

PORTER: Of course I don't agree. I couldn't read him then and I can't read him now. There was just one passage in a book called *Tender Is the Night*—I read that and thought, "Now I will read this again," because I couldn't be sure. Not only didn't I like his writing, but I didn't like the people he wrote about. I thought they weren't worth thinking about, and I still think so. It seems to me that your human beings have to have some kind of meaning. I just can't be interested in those perfectly stupid meaningless lives. And I don't like the same thing going on now—the way the artist simply will not face up to the final reckoning of things.

INTERVIEWER: In a philosophical sense?

PORTER: I'm thinking of it now in just the artistic sense— in the sense of an artist facing up to his own end meanings. I suppose I shouldn't be mentioning names, but I read a story some time ago, I think it was in the *Paris Review*, called "The McCabes."* Now I think William Styron is an extremely gifted man: he's very ripe and lush and with a kind of Niagara Falls of energy, and a kind of power. But he depends so on violence and a kind of exaggerated heat—at least it looks like heat, but just turns out to be summer lightning. Because there is nothing in the world more meaningless than that whole escapade of this man going off and winding up in the gutter. You sit back and think, "Well, let's see, where are we now?" All right, it's possible that that's just what Styron meant—the whole wicked pointlessness of things. But I tell you, nothing is pointless, and nothing is meaningless if the artist will face it. And it's his business to face it. He hasn't got the right to sidestep it like that. Human life itself may be almost pure chaos, but the work of the artist—the only thing he's good for—is to take these handfuls of confusion and disparate

---

*"The McCabes" was mistakenly not identified as a section from Styron's novel *Set This House on Fire*.

things, things that seem to be irreconcilable, and put them together in a frame to give them some kind of shape and meaning. Even if it's only his view of a meaning. That's what he's for—to give his view of life. Surely, we understand very little of what is happening to us at any given moment. But by remembering, comparing, waiting to know the consequences, we can sometimes see what an event really meant, what it was trying to teach us.

INTERVIEWER: You once said that every story begins with an ending, that until the end is known there is no story.

PORTER: That is where the artist begins to work: With the consequences of acts, not the acts themselves. Or the events. The event is important only as it affects your life and the lives of those around you. The reverberations, you might say, the overtones: that is where the artist works. In that sense it has sometimes taken me ten years to understand even a little of some important event that had happened to me. Oh, I could have given a perfectly factual account of what had happened, but I didn't know what it meant until I knew the consequences. If I didn't know the ending of a story, I wouldn't begin. I always write my last lines, my last paragraph, my last page first, and then I go back and work towards it. I know where I'm going. I know what my goal is. And how I get there is God's grace.

INTERVIEWER: That's a very classical view of the work of art—that it must end in resolution.

PORTER: Any true work of art has got to give you the feeling of reconciliation—what the Greeks would call catharsis, the purification of your mind and imagination—through an ending that is endurable because it is right and true. Oh, not in any pawky individual idea of morality or some parochial idea of right and wrong. Sometimes the end is very tragic, because it needs to be. One of the most perfect and marvelous endings in literature—it raises my hair now—is the little boy at the end of *Wuthering Heights,* crying that he's afraid to go across the moor because there's a man and woman walking there.

And there are three novels that I reread with pleasure and delight—three almost perfect novels, if we're talking about form, you know. One is *A High Wind in Jamaica* by

Richard Hughes, one is *A Passage to India* by E. M. Forster, and the other is *To the Lighthouse* by Virginia Woolf. Every one of them begins with an apparently insoluble problem, and every one of them works out of confusion into order. The material is all used so that you are going toward a goal. And that goal is the clearing up of disorder and confusion and wrong, to a logical and human end. I don't mean a happy ending, because after all at the end of *A High Wind in Jamaica* the pirates are all hanged and the children are all marked for life by their experience, but it comes out to an orderly end. The threads are all drawn up. I have had people object to Mr. Thompson's suicide at the end of *Noon Wine,* and I'd say, "All right, where was he going? Given what he was, his own situation, what else could he do?" Every once in a while when I see a character of mine just going towards perdition, I think, "Stop, stop, you can always stop and choose, you know." But no, being what he was, he already *has* chosen, and he can't go back on it now. I suppose the first idea that man had was the idea of fate, of the servile will, of a deity who destroyed as he would, without regard for the creature. But I think the idea of free will was the second idea.

INTERVIEWER: Has a story never surprised you in the writing? A character suddenly taken a different turn?

PORTER: Well, in the vision of death at the end of "Flowering Judas" I knew the real ending—that she was not going to be able to face her life, what she'd done. And I knew that the vengeful spirit was going to come in a dream to tow her away into death, but I didn't know until I'd written it that she was going to wake up saying, "No!" and be afraid to go to sleep again.

INTERVIEWER: That was, in a fairly literal sense, a "true" story, wasn't it?

PORTER: The truth is, I have never written a story in my life that didn't have a very firm foundation in actual human experience—somebody else's experience quite often, but an experience that became my own by hearing the story, by witnessing the thing, by hearing just a word perhaps. It doesn't matter, it just takes a little—a tiny seed. Then it takes root, and it grows. It's an organic thing. That story had been on my mind for years, growing out of this one little thing that happened in Mexico. It was forming and forming in my mind, until one night I was quite desperate. People are always so sociable, and I'm sociable too, and if I live around friends. . . . Well, they were insisting that I come and play bridge. But I was very firm, because I knew the time had come to write that story, and I had to write it.

INTERVIEWER: What was that "little thing" from which the story grew?

PORTER: Something I saw as I passed a window one evening. A girl I knew had asked me to come and sit with her, because a man was coming to see her, and she was a little afraid of him. And as I went through the courtyard, past the flowering judas tree, I glanced in the window and there she was sitting with an open book on her lap, and there was this great big fat man sitting beside her. Now Mary and I were friends, both American girls living in this revolutionary situation. She was teaching at an Indian school, and I was teaching dancing at a girls' technical school in Mexico City. And we were having a very strange time of it. I was more skeptical, and so I had already begun to look with a skeptical eye on a great many of the revolutionary leaders. Oh, the idea was all right, but a lot of men were misapplying it.

And when I looked through that window that evening, I saw something in Mary's face, something in her pose, something in the whole situation, that set up a commotion in my mind. Because until that moment I hadn't really understood that she was not able to take care of herself, because she was not able to face her own nature and was afraid of everything. I don't know why I saw it. I don't believe in intuition. When you get sudden flashes of perception, it is just the brain working faster than usual. But you've been getting ready to know it for a long time, and when it comes, you feel you've known it always.

INTERVIEWER: You speak of a story "forming" in your mind. Does it begin as a visual impression, growing to a narrative? Or how?

PORTER: All my senses were very keen, things came to me through my eyes, through all my pores. Everything hit me at once, you know. That makes it very difficult to describe just exactly what is happening. And then, I think the mind works in such a variety of ways. Sometimes an idea starts completely inarticulately. You're not thinking in images or words or—well, it's exactly like a dark cloud moving in your head. You keep wondering what will come out of this, and then it will dissolve itself into a set of—well, not images exactly, but really thoughts. You begin to think directly in words. Abstractly. Then the words transform themselves into images. By the time I write the story my people are up and alive and walking around and taking things into their own hands. They exist as independently inside my head as you do before me now. I have been criticized for not enough detail in describing my characters, and not enough furniture in the house. And the odd thing is that I see it all so clearly.

INTERVIEWER: What about the technical problems a story presents—its formal structure? How deliberate are you in matters of technique? For example, the use of the historical present in "Flowering Judas"?

PORTER: The first time someone said to me, "Why did you write 'Flowering Judas' in the historical present?" I thought for a moment and said, "Did I?" I'd never noticed it. Because I didn't *plan* to write it any way. A story forms in my mind and forms and forms, and when it's ready to go, I strike it down—it takes just the time I sit at the typewriter. I never think about form at all. In fact, I would say that I've never been interested in anything about writing after having learned, I hope, to write. That is, I mastered my craft as well as I could. There is a technique, there is a craft, and you have to learn it. Well, I did as well as I could with that, but now all in the world I am interested in is telling a story. I have something to tell you that I, for some reason, think is worth telling, and so I want to tell it as clearly and purely and simply as I can. But I had spent fifteen years at least learning to write. I practiced writing in every possible way that I could. I wrote a pastiche of other people, imitating Dr. Johnson and Laurence Sterne, and Petrarch and Shakespeare's sonnets, and then I tried writing my own way. I spent fifteen years learning to trust myself: that's what it comes to. Just as a pianist runs his scales for ten years before he gives his concert: because when he gives that concert, he can't be thinking of his fingering or of his hands; he has to be thinking of his interpretation, of the music he's playing. He's thinking of what he's trying to communicate. And if he hasn't got his technique perfected by then, he needn't give the concert at all.

INTERVIEWER: From whom would you say you learned most during this period of apprenticeship?

PORTER: The person who influenced me most, the real revelation in my life as a writer—though I don't write in the least like him—was Laurence Sterne, in *Tristram Shandy*. Why? Because, you know, I loved the grand style, and he made it look easy. The others, the great ones, really frightened me; they were so grand and magnificent they overawed me completely. But Laurence Sterne—well, it was just exactly as if he said, "Oh, come on, do it this way. It's so easy." So I tried to do it that way, and that taught me something, that taught me more than anybody else had. Because Laurence Sterne is a most complex and subtle man.

INTERVIEWER: What about your contemporaries? Did any of them contribute significantly to your development as a writer?

PORTER: I don't think I learned very much from my contemporaries. To begin with, we were all such individuals, and we were all so argumentative and so bent on our own courses that although I got a kind of support and personal friendship from my contemporaries, I didn't get very much help. I didn't show my work to anybody. I didn't hand it around among my friends for criticism, because, well, it just didn't occur to me to do it. Just as I didn't even try to publish anything until quite late because I didn't think I was ready. I published my first story in 1923. That was "María Concepción," the first story I ever finished. I rewrote "María Concepción" fifteen or sixteen times. That was a real battle, and I was thirty-three years old. I think it is the most curious lack of judgment to publish before you are ready. If there are echoes of other people in your work, you're not ready. If anybody has to help you rewrite your story, you're not ready. A story should be a finished work before it is shown. And after that, I will not allow anyone to change anything, and I will not change anything on anyone's advice. "Here is my story. It's a finished story. Take it or leave it!"

INTERVIEWER: You are frequently spoken of as a stylist. Do you think a style can be cultivated, or at least refined?

PORTER: I've been called a stylist until I really could tear my hair out. And I simply don't believe in style. The style is you. Oh, you can cultivate a style, I suppose, if you like. But I should say it remains a cultivated style. It remains artificial and imposed, and I don't think it deceives anyone. A cultivated style would be like a mask. Everybody knows it's a mask, and sooner or later you must show yourself—or at least, you show yourself as someone who could not afford to show himself, and so created something to hide behind. Style is the man. Aristotle said it first, as far as I know, and everybody has said it since, because it is one of those unarguable truths. You do not create a style. You work, and develop yourself; your style is an emanation from your own being. Symbolism is the same way. I never consciously took or adopted a symbol in my life. I certainly did not say, "This blooming tree upon which Judas is supposed to have hanged himself is going to be the center of my story." I named "Flowering Judas" after it was written, because when reading back over it I suddenly saw the whole symbolic plan and pattern of which I was totally unconscious while I was writing. There's a pox of symbolist theory going the rounds these days in American colleges in the writing courses. Miss Mary McCarthy, who is one of the wittiest and most acute and in some ways the worst-tempered woman in American letters, tells about a little girl who came to her with a story. Now Miss McCarthy is an extremely good critic, and she found this to be a good story, and she told the girl that it was—that she considered it a finished work, and that she could with a clear conscience go on to something else. And the little girl said, "But Miss McCarthy, my writing teacher said, 'Yes, it's a good piece of work, but now we must go back and put in the symbols!'" I think that's an amusing story, and it makes my blood run cold.

INTERVIEWER: But certainly one's command of the language can be developed and refined?

PORTER: I love the purity of language. I keep cautioning my students and anyone who will listen to me not to use the jargon of trades, not to use scientific language, because they're going to be out of date the day after tomorrow. The scientists change their vocabulary, their jargon, every day. So do the doctors, and the politicians, and the theologians—every body, every profession, every trade changes its vocabulary all of the time. But there is a basic pure human speech that exists in every language. And that is the language of the poet and the writer. So many words that had good meanings once upon a time have come to have meanings almost evil—certainly shabby, certainly inaccurate. And "psychology" is one of them. It has been so abused. This awful way a whole segment, not a generation but too many of the young writers, have got so soaked in the Freudian and post-Freudian vocabulary that they can't speak—not only can't speak English, but they can't speak *any* human language anymore. You can't write about people out of textbooks, and you can't use a jargon. You have to speak clearly and simply and purely in a language that a six-year-old child can understand; and yet have the meanings and the overtones of language, and the implications, that appeal to the highest intelligence—that is, the highest intelligence that one is able to reach. I'm not sure that I'm able to appeal to the highest intelligence, but I'm willing to try.

INTERVIEWER: You speak of the necessity of writing out of your own understanding rather than out of textbooks, and I'm sure any writer would agree. But what about the creation of masculine characters then? Most women writers, even the best of them like George Eliot, have run aground there. What about you? Was Mr. Thompson, say, a more difficult imaginative problem than Miranda?

PORTER: I never did make a profession of understanding people, man or woman or child, and the only thing I know about people is exactly what I have learned from the people right next to me. I have always lived in my immediate circumstances, from day to day. And when men ask me how I know so much about men, I've got a simple answer: everything I know about men, I've learned from men. If there is such a thing as a man's mind and a woman's mind—and I'm sure there is—it isn't what most critics mean when they talk about the two. If I show wisdom, they say I have a masculine mind. If I am silly and irrelevant—and Edmund Wilson says I often am—why then they say I have a typically feminine mind! (That's one thing about reaching my age: you can always quote the authorities about what you are.) But I haven't ever found it unnatural to be a woman.

INTERVIEWER: But haven't you found that being a woman presented to you, as an artist, certain special problems? It seems to me that a great deal of the upbringing of women encourages the dispersion of the self in many small bits, and that the practice of any kind of art demands a corralling and concentrating of that self and its always insufficient energies.

PORTER: I think that's very true and very right. You're brought up with the notion of feminine chastity and inaccessibility, yet with the curious idea of feminine availability in all spiritual ways, and in giving service to anyone who demands it. And I suppose that's why it has taken me twenty years to write this novel; it's been interrupted by just anyone who could jimmy his way into my life.

INTERVIEWER: Hemingway said once that a writer writes best when he's in love.

PORTER: I don't know whether you write better, but you feel so good you *think* you're writing better! And certainly love does create a rising of the spirit that makes everything you do seem easier and happier. But there must come a time when you no longer depend upon it, when the mind—not the will, really, either—takes over.

INTERVIEWER: In judging that the story is ready? You said a moment ago that the actual writing of a story is always done in a single spurt of energy—

PORTER: I always write a story in one sitting. I started "Flowering Judas" at seven p.m. and at one-thirty I was standing on a snowy windy corner putting it in the mailbox. And when I wrote my short novels, two of them, I just simply took the manuscript, packed a suitcase and departed to an inn in Georgetown, Pennsylvania, without leaving any forwarding address! Fourteen days later I had finished *Old Mortality* and *Noon Wine*.

INTERVIEWER: But the new novel *Ship of Fools* has been in the writing since 1942. The regime for writing this must have been a good deal different.

PORTER: Oh, it was. I went up and sat nearly three years in the country, and while I was writing it I worked every day, anywhere from three to five hours. Oh, it's true I used to do an awful lot of just sitting there thinking what comes next, because this is a great big unwieldy book with an enormous cast of characters—it's four hundred of my manuscript pages, and I can get four hundred and fifty words on a page. But all that time in Connecticut, I kept myself free for work; no telephone, no visitors—oh, I really lived like a hermit, everything but being fed through a grate! But it is, as Yeats said, a "solitary sedentary trade." And I did a lot of gardening, and cooked my own food, and listened to music, and of course I would read. I was really very happy. I can live a solitary life for months at a time, and it does me good, because I'm working. I just get up bright and early—sometimes at five o'clock—have my black coffee, and go to work.

INTERVIEWER: You work best in the morning, then?

PORTER: I work whenever I'm let. In the days when I was taken up with everything else, I used to do a day's work, or housework, or whatever I was doing, and then work at night. I worked when I could. But I prefer to get up very early in the morning and work. I don't want to speak to anybody or see anybody. Perfect silence. I work until the vein is out. There's something about the way you feel, you know when the well is dry, that you'll have to wait till tomorrow and it'll be full up again.

INTERVIEWER: The important thing, then, is to avoid any breaks or distractions while you're writing?

PORTER: To keep at a boiling point. So that I can get up in the morning with my mind still working where it was yesterday. Then I can stop in the middle of a paragraph and finish it the next day. I began writing *Ship of Fools* twenty years ago, and I've been away from it for several years at a time and stopped in the middle of a paragraph—but, you know, I can't tell where the crack is mended, and I hope nobody else can.

INTERVIEWER: You find no change in style, or in attitudes, over the years?

PORTER: It's astonishing how little I've changed: nothing in my point of view or my way of feeling. I'm going back now to finish some of the great many short stories that I have begun and not been able to finish for one reason or another. I've found one that I think I can finish. I have three versions of it: I started it in 1923, and it's based on an episode in my life that took place when I was twenty. Now here I am, seventy, and it's astonishing how much it's like me now. Oh, there are certain things, certain turns of sentence, certain phrases that I think I can sharpen and make more clear, more simple and direct, but my point of view, my being, is strangely unchanged. We change, of course, every day; we are not the same people who sat down at this table, yet there is a basic and innate being that is unchanged.

INTERVIEWER: *Ship of Fools* too is based upon an event that took place ten years or more before the first writing, isn't it? A sea voyage just before the beginning of the European war.

PORTER: It is the story of my first voyage to Europe in 1931. We embarked on an old German ship at Vera Cruz and we landed in Bremerhaven twenty-eight days later. It was a crowded ship, a great mixture of nationalities, religions, political beliefs—all that sort of thing. I don't think I spoke a half-dozen words to anybody. I just sat there and watched—not deliberately, though. I kept a diary in the form of a letter to a friend, and after I got home the friend sent it back. And, you know, it is astonishing what happened on that boat, and what happened in my mind afterwards. Because it is fiction now.

INTERVIEWER: The title—isn't it from a medieval emblem?—suggests that it might also be an allegory.

PORTER: It's just exactly what it seems to be. It's an allegory if you like, though I don't think much of the allegorical as a standard. It's a parable, if you like, of the ship of this world on its voyage to eternity.

INTERVIEWER: I remember your writing once—I think in the preface to "Flowering Judas"—of an effort to understand what

you called the "majestic and terrible failure" of Western man.
You were speaking then of the World War and what it signified
of human folly. It seems to me that *Ship of Fools* properly belongs to that investigation of betrayal and self-delusion—

PORTER: Betrayal and treachery, but also self-betrayal and
self-deception—the way that all human beings deceive themselves about the way they operate. . . . There seems to be a
kind of order in the universe, in the movement of the stars and
the turning of the earth and the changing of the seasons, and
even in the cycle of human life. But human life itself is almost
pure chaos. Everyone takes his stance, asserts his own rights
and feelings, mistaking the motives of others, and his own. . . .
Now, nobody knows the end of the life he's living, and neither
do I. Don't forget I am a passenger on that ship; it's not the
other people altogether who are the fools! We don't really know
what is going to happen to us, and we don't know why. Quite
often the best we can do is to keep our heads, and try to keep
at least one line unbroken and unobstructed. Misunderstand-
ing and separation are the natural conditions of man. We come
together only at these pre-arranged meeting grounds; we were
all passengers on that ship, yet at his destination, each one
was alone.

INTERVIEWER: Did you find that the writing of *Ship of Fools*
differed from the writing of shorter fiction?

PORTER: It's just a longer voyage, that's all. It was the question
of keeping everything moving at once. There are about forty-
five main characters, all taking part in each others' lives, and
then there was a steerage of sugar workers, deportees. It was
all a matter of deciding which should come first, in order to
keep the harmonious moving forward. A novel is really like a
symphony, you know, where instrument after instrument has
to come in at its own time, and no other. I tried to write it as a
short novel, you know, but it just wouldn't confine itself. I
wrote notes and sketches. And finally I gave in. "Oh, no, this
is simply going to have to be a novel," I thought. That was a
real horror. But it needed a book to contain its full movement:
of the sea, and the ship on the sea, and the people going
around the deck, and into the ship, and up from it. That whole
movement, felt as one forward motion: I can feel it while I'm
reading it. I didn't "intend" it, but it took hold of me.

INTERVIEWER: As writing itself, perhaps, "took hold" of you—we began by your saying that you had never intended to be a professional anything, even a professional writer.

PORTER: I look upon literature as an art, and I practice it as an art. Of course, it is also a vocation, and a trade, and a profession, and all kinds of things; but first it's an art, and you should practice it as that, I think. I know a great many people disagree, and they are welcome to it. I think probably the important thing is to get your work done, in the way you can—and we all have our different and separate ways. But I look upon literature as an art, and I believe that if you misuse it or abuse it, it will leave you. It is not a thing that you can nail down and use as you want. You have to let it use you, too.

❑ Critical Essays

◻ RAY B. WEST, JR. ■

Katherine Anne Porter: Symbol and Theme in "Flowering Judas"

Katherine Anne Porter, in writing of Katherine Mansfield's fictional method in 1937, said that she "states no belief, gives no motive, airs no theories, but simply presents to the reader a situation, a place and a character, and there it is; and the emotional content is present as implicitly as the germ in the grain of wheat." Of her own method she has written: "Now and again thousands of memories converge, harmonize, arrange themselves around a central idea in a coherent form, and I write a story."

Enlightening though these statements are concerning Miss Porter's concept of a short story, true as they appear to be of her own fiction and of the creative process, they still leave the reader with his own problem of "understanding" when he is confronted with the individual story. If we disregard the fact that the first statement was made about a fellow artist (it is still descriptive of Miss Porter's own stories), we must yet discover the "germ" which produced the emotion and which flowers into the final form of the story. Though we might say that the converging, the harmonizing, and the arranging constitute a logical, though partly subconscious, activity which serves to bring the objects of memory into some kind of order, still it is the nature of the synthesis—particularly in the predominantly social themes from *Flowering Judas* (1930) to *The Leaning Tower* (1944)—which puzzles most readers.

That Miss Porter herself was aware of the nature of her sensibility is clear from her comments concerning Miranda in

From *Accent* 7 (Spring 1947): 182–188.

a late story, who had, she says, "a powerful social sense, which was like a fine set of antennae radiating from every pore of her skin." Miss Porter's own social sense is most obvious (perhaps too obvious) in her latest long story, "The Leaning Tower," but it is not with the most obvious examples that the reader wishes to concern himself; rather, with the seemingly obscure; and since I have nowhere seen published or heard expounded an examination of "Flowering Judas," and since it is perhaps Miss Porter's best known story (to my mind, her most successful single work of fiction), let us examine that with the aim of understanding just what the author means by social sensibility—how it operates within the story itself.

The surface detail in "Flowering Judas" is relatively simple. An American girl who has been educated in a Southern convent is in Mexico teaching school and aiding a group of revolutionaries under Braggioni, a sensual hulk of a man, formerly a starving poet, but who is now in a position to indulge even his appetite for the most expensive of small luxuries. The girl (Laura) teaches her children in the daytime and at night runs errands for Braggioni, acting as a go-between for him and the foreign revolutionaries, delivering messages and narcotics to members of the party who are in jail. At the point where the story opens, Braggioni has come to Laura's apartment to discover, if possible, whether it would be worth the effort to attempt an assault upon her "notorious virginity," which he, like the others, cannot understand. Laura is physically attractive, and this is not the first time that she has been courted by the Mexicans. Her first suitor was a young captain whom she evaded by spurring her horse when he attempted to take her into his arms, pretending that the horse had suddenly shied. The second was a young organizer of the typographers' union who had serenaded her and written her bad poetry which he tacked to her door. She had unwittingly encouraged him by tossing a flower from her balcony as he sang to her from the patio. A third person, Eugenio, is unknown to the reader until near the end of the story, when it turns out that he is expected to die of a self-imposed overdose of the narcotics which Laura had delivered to him at the prison. He is, however, the principal figure in a dream which ends the story, a dream in which Laura imagines him to have accused her of murdering him and in which he forces her to eat of the blossoms of the Judas tree which grows in the courtyard below her window.

All of the immediate action takes place in Laura's apartment after she has returned and found Braggioni awaiting her. He sings to her in a voice "passionately off key," talks about their curious relationship, about the revolution, and finally leaves after having Laura clean his pistol for use in a May-day disturbance between the revolutionaries and the Catholics of a near-by town. Braggioni returns to his wife, whom he has deserted for a month to pay attention to Laura, and who, despite the fact that she has been weeping over his absence, accepts his return gratefully and washes his feet. Laura goes to bed and has her dream of Eugenio.

It will be seen, even from this brief summary, that there are a great many details unexplained by the course of the action. There is the concern with revolutionary activities running throughout; there are the comments concerning Laura's religious training: the nun-like clothing, her slipping away into a small church to pray, the May-day demonstration. Obviously, a great many details have symbolic references, not least of which is the title itself.

If we turn to any standard encyclopedia, we discover that the Flowering Judas is a tree commonly known as the Judas tree or Red-bud. We learn further that a popular legend relates that it is from this tree that Judas Iscariot hanged himself. A second fact is that the exact title appears in a line from T. S. Eliot's poem "Gerontion":

> In the juvescence of the year
> Came Christ the tiger

> In depraved May, dogwood and chestnut, flowering judas,
> To be eaten, to be divided, to be drunk
> Among whispers.

This is scarcely a coincidence, since Eliot's passage so clearly suggests Laura's activity at the end of the story. Our first question is: what use is made of this symbol? The dividing, the eating and drinking among whispers suggests the

Christian sacrament, but it is a particular kind of sacrament. "Christ the tiger" refers to the pagan ritual in which the blood of a slain tiger is drunk in order to engender in the participants the courage of the tiger heart. In a sense this is only a more primitive form of sacrament, one which presupposes a *direct* rather than symbolic transfer of virtues from the animal to man. In the Christian ritual, the symbolic blood of Christ is drunk in remembrance of atonement; that is, symbolically to engender the virtues of Christ in the participant.

If the Judas tree, then, is a symbol for the betrayer of Christ (the legend says that its buds are red because it actually became the body of Judas, who is said to have had red hair), then the sacrament in which Laura participated—the eating of the buds of the Flowering Judas—is a sacrament, not of remembrance, but of betrayal.

This leads us to other uses of the Saviour-symbol in the story. The first is Braggioni, who, at one point, is even called a "world-saviour." It is said that "his skin has been punctured in honorable warfare"; "he has a real mobility; a love of humanity raised above mere personal affections"; finally, he is depicted, like Christ, undergoing the final purification, the foot-washing. But there are important reservations in the use of this symbol: (1) the note of irony with which Braggioni is depicted and which suggests the attitude the reader should take toward him; (2) each time the Christ-like epithet is used, it is accompanied by other, non-Christian characteristics: "His skin has been *punctured* in honorable warfare, but *he is a skilled revolutionary*"; he is a *professional* lover of humanity, a *hungry* world-saviour. It is the use of the religious symbols alongside the secular which makes Braggioni the complex and interesting character that he is.

The second use of the Christ-symbol is present in the character of Eugenio, who is seen first as one of the revolutionary workers languishing in jail, but who figures most prominently as the person in Laura's dream. His name contains the clue to his symbolic meaning—well-born. As Christ is the Son of God, he is well-born. He is, likewise, a symbol of all mankind—Man. We say he is the "Son of Man." In this respect, Eugenio is also Christ-like, for he is well-born without the reservations noted in the character of Braggioni—in the highest sense. And as Judas was the direct cause of Christ's

92

crucifixion, so Laura becomes the murderer of Eugenio (of Man) by carrying narcotics to his prison cell, the narcotics through which he (Christ-like) surrendered himself up to death.

We can say, then, that the use of religious symbolism by Miss Porter might suggest that her story be taken as a kind of religious allegory. But there are other, complicating symbols. There is, for instance, Laura's fear of machines such as the *automobile;* there is her dislike for things made on *machines;* and finally there is the statement that *the machine is sacred* to the workers. In the last instance, we may see how the word "machine" is coupled with the religious word "sacred," thus bringing the two kinds of symbols into juxtaposition, just as the same thing is implied in the descriptions we have had of Braggioni. For instance, "His skin has been punctured in honorable warfare" suggests the act of crucifixion, but "puncture" is not a word which we would ordinarily use in describing either the nailing of Christ to the cross or the piercing of his flesh by the spear of the Roman soldier. The most common use of "puncture" now is its reference to automobile tires (of which Laura is afraid). Likewise, the word "professional" used to modify "a lover of humanity" brings the modern idea of business efficiency into conjunction with the image of Christ, as though one were to say, explicitly: "Braggioni is an impersonal, cold-blooded Christ."

A third type of symbols is composed of love-symbols (erotic, secular, and divine). The story shows Laura unable to participate in love upon any of the levels suggested: (1) as a divine lover in the Christian sense, for it is clear that she is incapable of divine passion when she occasionally sneaks into a small church to pray; (2) as a professional lover in the sense that Braggioni is one, for she cannot participate in the revolutionary fervor of the workers, which might be stated as an activity expressive of secular love for their fellow men; she cannot even feel the proper emotion for the children who scribble on their blackboards, "We lov ar ticher"; (3) as an erotic lover, for she responds to none of her three suitors, though she thoughtlessly throws one of them a rose (the symbol of erotic love), an act of profanation, since the boy wears it in his hat until it withers and dies.

Having located these symbols, it is now our problem to

examine the use that is made of them. More specifically, we can say that the religious symbols represent the Christian ideology, while the secular are symbols most readily identified with the attitudes of Marxism. As philosophy, they would seem to represent the two most extreme positions possible; yet both claim as their aim the betterment of mankind. If we consider them as areas within which man may act, we might represent them as two circles.

The third field (love) is not so much an area within which man performs as it is an attitude toward his actions. The fact that we refer to "divine love" and "secular love" will illustrate this distinction. On the other hand, if we speak of a "code of love," then love comes to resemble a kind of philosophy and is similar to Christianity and Marxism. As there is evidence in the relationship of Laura to the young Captain and to her suitor from the typographers' union that Miss Porter had this relationship in mind as well as the other, we might represent our third symbolic field as a circle overlapping the other two, but also existing as a separate area.

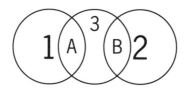

At this point, we must remember the relationship between "Flowering Judas" and Eliot's "Gerontion." The poem is concerned with a wasteland image; that is, with a view of life as a wasteland, sterile and barren as old-age, because of the absence of any fructifying element. Eliot's old man in the poem says:

> I have lost my passion: why should I need to keep it
> Since what is kept must be adulterated?

I have lost my sight, smell, hearing, taste, and touch:
How should I use them for your closer contact?

In "Flowering Judas" Laura has lost the use of her senses: when the children scribble their message of love, she can feel nothing for them. They are only "wise, innocent, clay-colored faces," just as the revolutionists have become "clay masks with the power of human speech." She is like the prisoners, shut off from human contact, who, when they complain to her, "'Dear little Laura, time doesn't pass in this infernal hole, and I won't know when it is time to sleep unless I have a reminder,' she brings them their favorite narcotics, and says in a tone that does not wound them with pity, 'Tonight will really be night for you.'" Seeing the colored flowers the children have painted, she remembers the young captain who has made love to her and thinks, "I must send him a box of colored crayons." She confuses the children with the prisoners, "The poor prisoners who come every day bringing flowers to their jailor." "It is monstrous," she thinks with sudden insight, "to confuse love with revolution, night with day, life with death." Laura, like the figure in Eliot's poem, has lost her passion, she has lost her sight, smell, hearing, taste, and touch. She cannot use them for closer contact.

Now, if we return to our circles, perhaps this can be made clear. The philosophical systems represented by each circle (1. religion. 2. revolution. 3. love) represent a means of dealing with the wasteland. That is, faith in any one of the systems will provide a kind of signpost, which is the first step in transforming the wilderness of modern social living. By observing the sign-posts, we at least know where we are going or what we are doing there. Yet—it is still the wasteland. However, when we superimpose circle 3 upon either of the other two, the sterility disappears. In other words, either orthodox religion or socialism is a wasteland until transformed by the fructifying power of love; obversely, love is impossible without the object provided by either. In terms of our diagram, all is sterility outside the circles or at any point within the circles where 3 does not overlap either 1 or 2—that is, within the areas A or B.

Laura may be said to be outside any of the circles. Because of her training, she is pulled away from a belief in the revolutionary cause of Braggioni. Because of her desire to accept the principles of revolution, she is unable to accept the principles of her religious education. Without either Christianity or Marxism, it is impossible for her to respond to her suitors or to the children. She cannot even feel pity for the prisoners; she can only supply them with narcotics, which likens their condition to hers, for her life seems to be a senseless kind of existence similar to the drugged sleep of the prisoners.

Braggioni's condition is likened to Laura's ("We are more alike than you realize in some things," he tells her), but there are two important differences: (1) he has the revolutionary ideal as a guide; (2) he is capable of redemption, as the final, footwashing scene with his wife ("whose sense of reality is beyond criticism") shows. We can say, then, that Braggioni is not, as Laura is, outside the circles. He is within one of them, but it is not until he is touched with pity that he is brought wholly within the area of redemption (either A or B). Laura is not redeemed, even though she desires it, as the eating of the buds of the Judas tree suggests. Her sacrament is a devouring gesture and Eugenio calls her a cannibal, because she is devouring him (Man). She is, like Judas, the betrayer; and her betrayal, like his, consisted in an inability to believe. Without faith she is incapable of passion, thence of love, finally of life itself. Reduced to the inadequacy of statement, we might say that the theme, lacking all of the story's subtle comment, might be rendered as: Man cannot live divided by materialistic and spiritual values, nor can he live in the modern world by either without faith and love.

As the Nazi landlady in "The Leaning Tower" is made to say when overcharging the American student who wishes to cancel his lease: "Indecision is a very expensive luxury."

Laura's world, then, is as barren and sterile as the world of Eliot's "Gerontion"; it is a living death. Said another way, the living world exists only in our sensory perception of it, and any deadening of the senses (through a denial of traditional human values) constitutes a relinquishing of moral responsibility—the betrayal of mankind into the hands of the Braggionis or, as in "The Leaning Tower," into the hands of the Nazis.

This is, I suspect, what one reviewer discovered as early as 1938, when, in a review of the volume *Flowering Judas,* he wrote: "Miss Porter, I feel, is one of the most 'socially conscious' of our writers." But one might also fear that this reviewer was thinking in terms of the predominant Marxist movements of the thirties, into none of which Miss Porter could, obviously, be made to fit. "I do not mean," he continued, "simply that she is conscious of the physical suffering of her impoverished people; I mean rather that she understands the impoverishment of mind and spirit which accompanies the physical fact, and she sees too that some native goodness in these minds and spirits still lives."

But if "some native goodness" were all Miss Porter's characters had to recommend themselves to us as resolutions of our social dilemma, then every author who does not allegorize good and evil is still "socially conscious," and the reviewer's remarks represent a somewhat dubious compliment. The fact is, however, that he was right perceptually. Behind Miss Porter's elaborate structure of symbol and myth lies the psychological motivation which produces the theme. The germ which lies implicit in the grain of wheat is the central idea about which her memories cluster. An idea does not constitute her "meaning" in the usual sense of the word, but it represents a concept which makes the surface detail available to meaning. To put it another way, the very rightness of the *ideological* fact (the myth or symbol) charges the *particular* fact (the object as it exists in nature) with a meaning that is presented as an experiential whole, but which is available in all its complex relationships only when we have become aware of the entire field of reference.

☐ LEON GOTTFRIED ■

Death's Other Kingdom: Dantesque and Theological Symbolism in "Flowering Judas"

I

> I have a great deal of religious symbolism in my stories
> because I have a very deep sense of religion and also I
> have a religious training. And I suppose you don't invent‎
> symbolism. You don't say, "I'm going to have the flower-
> ing judas tree stand for betrayal," but, of course, it does.
> —KATHERINE ANNE PORTER[1]

The attempt to portray hell and its leading personages by re-
lating them parodically to heaven using inversions of varying
degrees of complexity is traditional. Scholastic theologians
like St. Thomas regularly related the various virtues and kinds
of blessedness to their opposites, and both Dante and Milton,
the two greatest poetic infernologists, made systematic use of
parody and ironic parallelism. Katherine Anne Porter is clearly
working in this ironic mode in "Flowering Judas," a story dealing with latter-day lost souls. Her nun-like heroine is a lapsed
devotee of the religion of revolution. She refers to the religion
of the machine and uses a parodic saviour and symbolic per-
versions of the sacrament of communion and the purification
ceremony of foot-washing. Precautions must be observed, however. Porter is neither a theologian nor a theological poet like
Dante. In most of her other works there is comparatively little
explicit use of the religious and eschatological diction and imagery so prevalent in "Flowering Judas." Even taking the word
in the most extended sense, one would be unlikely to call her

From *PMLA* 84 (1969): 112–124.

a "religious" writer in the sense that T. S. Eliot or Francois Mauriac were religious writers.

The principal difference that sets her apart from the "religious" writers is not the fact that in most of her work she has not used the elaborate system of religious allusions prominent in "Flowering Judas." Rather, it is that her portrayal of hell (not only in "Flowering Judas") is without reference to any corresponding "heaven" or system of ultimate values other than those of Catholicism and Marxism, both discredited. In this respect she is a typical modern secular writer for whom meaning and value are created, not given; she enacts the characteristic doom of the modern Promethean artist struggling to carve out of the chaos of experience some order or meaning which can come into existence, if at all, only after the struggle. In her 1940 "Introduction" she calls the stories in *Flowering Judas and Other Stories* "fragments of a much larger plan," a plan which never fully materialized. "They are," she goes on, "what I was then able to achieve in the way of order and form and statement in a period of grotesque dislocations in a whole society where the world was heaving in the sickness of a millennial change." For herself, she says, "most of the energies of my mind and spirit have been spent in the effort . . . to understand the logic of this majestic and terrible failure of the life of man in the Western world." Admitting that the voice of the individual artist in such times may seem inconsequential, she nevertheless concludes with a triumphant statement of faith in art itself:

> The arts do live continuously, and they live literally by faith; their names and their shape and their uses and their basic meanings survive unchanged in all that matters through times of interruption, diminishment, neglect; they outlive governments and creeds and the societies, even the very civilizations that produced them. They cannot be destroyed altogether because they represent the substance of faith and the only reality. They are what we find again when the ruins are cleared away.

Although Porter is referring specifically to the period of the two world wars, she is speaking of art in a way that might have met with ready understanding and approval any time these three hundred years or more, and assuredly for the last century and a half, and she speaks of it in much the same religious tone used by T. S. Eliot to urge the necessity of keeping alive another sort of faith during what he believed to be our spiritual Dark Ages. But faith in the vitality and reality of art itself ("the only reality") is not at all the same as faith in the existence of an order or spirit informing that other "reality" of which art has commonly been held to be a reflection. In Porter's writing, such an order is implicit only by absence or negation. Yet, in her story of the failure of a young woman involved in the materialistic revolutionary movement in Mexico of the 1920s, Porter's early training and background offered her a rich store of religious imagery and language, behind which lie centuries of systematic theological thought, to give order and form to one of her sketches of the "failure of the life of man in the Western world."

II

> I know thy works, that thou art neither cold nor hot:
> I would thou wert cold or hot.
> So then because thou art lukewarm, and neither cold nor
> hot, I will spue thee out of my mouth.
> —Rev.3.15—16

In "Flowering Judas," as in a number of her other stories, Porter is concerned with the problem (or sin) of noninvolvement and the waste for which it is responsible. Among the many other writers who dealt with the theme of the half-alive spiritual state during the period between wars, perhaps the most influential was T. S. Eliot. It is therefore not surprising that we find Porter in "Flowering Judas" drawing, as did so many of her contemporaries, upon Eliot's poetry. Her story echoes Eliot's "Gerontion" in its title and in the use of the tree's blossoms as a substitute for the Host in a travesty of Christian communion. The landscape of the heroine's dream at the end of the story, in which the infernal communion takes place, is reminiscent of both "The Waste Land" and "The Hollow Men." Thematically the story has affinities with these poems, but "The Hollow Men" seems especially close in theme and imagery to the problems of Laura, Porter's heroine. Like the life-in-death of the hollow men, Laura's life is character-ized by "Shape without form, shade without colour,/Paralysed force, gesture without motion." Each of Eliot's negations is carried out in the imagery of Laura's story.

Behind both Eliot's hollow men (and much of his other poetry of this period) and Porter's Laura, who so much resembles them, lies the *Inferno* of Dante, especially the third canto, wherein is depicted the fate of the souls who were neither good nor evil, who had never truly lived—those "sorrowful souls" whose eternity is spent in aimless wandering in the vestibule of hell, as they had lived "without blame and without praise" (35–36). Central among these lost souls, and representative of their plight, is that of one (perhaps Pontius Pilate) "who, through cowardice, made the great denial." Negation or refusal or moral choice is the keynote of the spiritual existence of these creatures, as it was for Pilate, as it is for the hollow men, and as it has become for Laura. Feeling that "she has been betrayed irreparably by the disunion between her way of living and her feeling of what life should be," Laura has sought a point of fixity in commitment to the revolutionary cause, but her commitment is wholly outward: "she wears the uniform of an idea." Like the saint or mystic, "she is not at home in the world" and tries to persuade herself that her stoical denial of all external events "is a sign that she is gradually perfecting herself" in a spiritual discipline cultivated against some nameless, impending disaster. But her stoicism is a parody of the spiritual discipline of the saint or mystic, for her unworldliness is utterly dissociated from joy. Totally negative, it does not stem from feelings of kinship with anything beyond herself, but from "the very cells of her flesh [which] reject knowledge and kinship in one monotonous word. No. No. No."

Laura, to be sure, is not entirely "without praise." We are told that "all praise her gray eyes, and the soft, round under lip which promises gayety, yet is always grave." Nevertheless, "nobody touches her," and her greatest fame is for the "puzzle of her notorious virginity," a virginity whose quality is purely negative. But the thematic patterns of negation in the story are more complex than this, and far more complexly interwoven with Dantesque imagery. The ultimate refusal is that of life itself, and we are given an example in the suicide of Eugenio that seems the logical culmination of his meaningless, dope-sodden, imprisoned existence. His death was not a protest nor an act of pride, but it was in keeping with the general motif of *acedia* that dominates the story—he committed suicide "because he was bored."

Laura, the uninvolved, did nothing about it. "He refused to allow me to call the prison doctor," she says, though in his stupor he could not have prevented her from doing so. In Laura's dream at the end of the story, Eugenio appears to her, calls her murderer, and hands her "the warm and bleeding flowers" that he stripped from the Judas tree. As he holds them to her lips she becomes aware that he *is* the tree, "that his hand was fleshless, a cluster of small white petrified branches," and that she is eating his body and blood. While the image of bleeding and talking plants is familiar to readers of Virgil and Dante, the association with suicide is Dante's alone (*Inferno*, xiii). By misusing their freedom of bodily movement, the suicides have robbed themselves of their own form forever. They are pent up in trees and bushes and can find expression only in the agony of bleeding when some chance passerby such as Dante, or malicious creatures such as the Harpies, break leaves or branches from them. While they bleed they can speak. Porter blended the image from Dante with an image of infernal communion from Eliot's "Gerontion":

> In depraved May, dogwood and chestnut, flowering judas,
> To be eaten, to be divided, to be drunk
> Among whispers . . . ,

thus achieving a richly symbolic unifying statement that connects all the negations of life and love in Laura's story with the ultimate negation of life itself by self-destruction.

According to Dante, love is the spring of all spiritual (and, indeed, physical) motion. In *Purgatory* he has Virgil explain that neither the creator nor any creature is devoid of love (xvii. 91–92). But the whole of Dante's *Purgatory* is designed to show that our sins stem from three sorts of perversion of love: love of wrong objects, excessive love of proper but secondary objects, and deficiency of love (xvii. 96). The last vice is the way of the slothful, whose lack of diligence in pursuit of the good is the sin of *acedia*. Appropriately, it is on the cornice of the slothful in *Purgatory* that Virgil pauses to explain the doctrine of love and its relation to sin. In the *Inferno*, which is not organized according to the seven deadly sins, the slothful are given no distinct habitation, but may have some relationship to the *cattivi* of the Antinferno, the souls who were kin to those angels who were neither rebellious nor faithful to God, but were for themselves (iii. 38–39).

In "Flowering Judas," it is Laura's deficiency of love that Braggioni, her revolutionary leader, finds most difficult to understand. Braggioni himself is an evil soul who becomes positive at least by virtue of action, and he cannot see why Laura "works so hard for the revolutionary idea unless she loves some man who is in it. 'Are you not in love with someone?' 'No,' says Laura. 'And no one is in love with you?' 'No.' Then it is your own fault.'"

But to understand Laura more fully, we must direct our attention to Braggioni himself, who seems at so many points to be her opposite. Whereas she is prim in her blue serge dress and round white collar "not purposely nun-like" (it is "one of twenty precisely alike, folded in blue tissue paper in the upper drawer of her clothes chest"), he is resplendent in his expensive and gaudy dress. Whereas she is ascetic and notoriously chaste, he is a sensualist. He is frankly opportunistic, while "she has encased herself in a set of principles." She cannot love at all, but he loves himself with great "tenderness and amplitude and eternal charity." Yet in spite of these contrasts and more, Braggioni insists to Laura that "we are more alike than you realize in some things." Although she inwardly rejects the kinship, she admits to herself: "It may be true that I am as corrupt, in another way, as Braggioni, . . . as callous, as incomplete." If there is, indeed, such a similarity, where can it lie?

III

Amari habent iram permanentem propter permanentiam tristitiae, quam inter viscera tenent clausam . . .
[The sullen have a permanent anger because of a permanent sorrow which they hold closed up in their bowels.]
—THOMAS AQUINAS,
Summa Theologica, II–II, Q. 158, Art. 5

It is at once evident in "Flowering Judas" that Braggioni, though prideful and vainglorious, is preeminently a man of wrath, both by profession and inclination, and that his wrath is of the permanent sort stemming from a deep inner wound. St. Thomas, in describing the wrathful, follows Aristotle by distinguishing among three kinds: the quick-tempered (*acuti*), the vindictive (*difficiles*), and the sullen (*amari*). Dante consigns the souls of the sullen to the fifth circle of the *Inferno* (Canto vii) where they are permanently buried beneath the black slime of the sorrowful (*tristo*) Styx. Dante calls them "the sorrowful" (*tristi*), and he seems to echo Aquinas when he has them describe themselves as bearing within themselves their sluggish or slothful fume (*accidioso fummo*, vii. 123). Because they darkened the glad light of the sun and the sweet air with their sullenness, they now sadden themselves in the black muck (vii. 124). Completely submerged, they cannot communicate directly, but for the sake of his disciple, Virgil interprets the bubbles they make, commenting afterwards that this is the song they gurgle inwardly, in their throats (vii. 125). St. Thomas observes that all anger (*ira*) is compounded of the contrary passions of hope (of vengeance) and sorrow (on account of some pain that has been suffered) (I–II, Q. 46, Art. 1). As for the sullen specifically, he attributes the permanence of their anger to a permanent sorrow (*tristitia*) that they nurse inside themselves.

If we examine Braggioni, beginning with his description in the first paragraph of "Flowering Judas," certain details stand out. In the opening sentence we see him in an uncomfortable heap, singing in a "furry, mournful voice." Lately Laura has found him waiting for her every night with his "surly, waiting expression . . . snarling a tune under his breath." Unaware in his vanity of his "miserable performance" as a singer, he refuses Laura's offer of the brown beverage chocolate, for it "thickens the voice." A few pages further on, he is described as singing another song "with tremendous emphasis, weighing his words," in sharp and perhaps ironic contrast to his normal style that is like the muddy gurgling of Dante's *tristi* who cannot speak whole words (vii. 126) because of their situation. His song is a melancholy ditty in which the singer complains of his utter loneliness with no one to console him. He finds a clear singing voice, it seems, only to indulge his meaningless and self-pitying sorrow.

It is not long before his self-pity and melancholy find speech, as he tells Laura, in language suggesting both the Psalmist (Psalms lxix.2, 21) and Christ: "It is true everything turns to dust in the hand, to gall on the tongue." In his abiding *tristitia,* this secular savior recalls by travesty Isaiah's "man of sorrows, and acquainted with grief." Like the Biblical man of sorrows, Braggioni assuredly "hath no form nor comeliness." Isaiah's servant of the Lord "was wounded for our transgressions," and Braggioni sees himself as "wounded by life" (Isaiah liii.2–5). In spite of his unrestrained self-indulgence, nothing satisfies him. "I am disappointed in everything as it comes. Everything," he sighs. At this point he affirms his kinship with Laura: "You, poor thing, you will be disappointed too. You are born for it. We are more alike than you realize in some things. Wait and see."

Braggioni's grotesque melancholy is at last appeased when he returns to his long-suffering wife. She calls him her "angel" and washes his feet in a parody of Christian ritual. In his softened and sentimental mood, "he is sorry for everything and bursts into tears. 'Ah, yes, I am hungry, I am tired, let us eat something together,' he says between sobs." He enjoys the luxury of sobbing with his wife, who is represented as a *mater dolorosa,* endlessly weeping. She begs her idol to forgive her, "and this time he is refreshed by the solemn, endless rain of her tears."

Laura's stern self-control may seem at the opposite pole from the maudlin emotionalism of Braggioni, but she appears to share with him an abiding sorrow. She denies life, hiding her vital body with its "long, invaluably beautiful legs" and its "great round breasts . . . like a nursing mother's" in ascetic, nun-like garb, just as she has encased her soul in "the uniform of an idea." Braggioni is a minister of death, consecrated to an apocalypse of "gaping trenches, of crashing walls and broken bodies." He reserves his love for pistols and cannon and his faith for dynamite. He is an embodiment of St. Paul's warning against excessive sorrow, for "the sorrow of the world worked death" (II Cor., vii.10). Laura recognizes this as she hands him his gunbelt, saying: "Put that on, and go kill somebody in Morelia, and you will be happier." Braggioni, the wrathful, with his infinite love and charity for himself, is a worker of death, but Laura oils and loads his pistols. She lacks love even for herself. She is allied to death through her passiveness and through the self-delusion in which she monstrously confuses "love with revolution, night with day, life with death." She may abstractly love the "tender round hands" of the pupils in the school where she teaches, but they "remain strangers to her."

Braggioni is guilty of every sin, but Laura is virtuous only by negation, not by attachment to any good: "Denying everything, she may walk anywhere in safety, she looks at everything without amazement." Her "bold talismanic word" *No* serves her in place of the Lord's prayer, for it "does not suffer her to be led into evil." Her deficiency of love renders her the victim of that spiritual sloth of *acedia* that Thomas Aquinas calls sorrow in the face of spiritual good (II–II, Q. 35, Art. 2). If we accept the association of *acedia* with Dante's *cattivi*, we see, also, that the poet denies even a total death to the souls who die confirmed in this sin. The souls of the uninvolved in Dante are rejected by both Heaven and Hell, where the damned might have some glory over them, just as Laura lives in Mexico but is not accepted by it ("I am tempted to forgive you for being a *gringa*," says Braggioni).

Laura, who is so frightened of life, is equally frightened of death. Although she "may walk anywhere in safety," she is possessed by what may not be a wholly irrational fear "that violence, mutilation, a shocking death, wait for her." She translates this "warning in her blood" into homely terms by taking excessive precautions when crossing streets, so as not to be killed by an automobile. She has devoted herself to a cause which promised men that they might have life more abundantly only to find herself an agent of the forces of death, a cause that seemed to offer an earthly fulfillment of charity only to discover that it is riddled with intrigue, jealousy, and selfishness. Braggioni's "gluttonous bulk," so different from the "vessel of abstract virtues" she had imagined the ideal revolutionist to be, becomes the "symbol of her many disillusions." The life more abundant has become a "feeding trough" for him and other envious "hungry world-saviours." But in spite of her disillusion, Laura is paralyzed. She "feels herself bogged in a nightmare." Incapable of loving either man or God, she has no positive good to which she can turn and so remains motionless, the unwilling but unrejecting agent of death. Charity is travestied in her routine, abstract attachment to the class of children she teaches and in her distribution of narcotics to the prisoners in the "infernal hole" of their prison, the narcotics that Eugenio employs to kill himself. It is not irrelevant that St. Thomas calls *acedia* a vice directly opposed to the theological virtue of charity (II–II, Q. 35, Art. 2).

It is clear on both psychological and theological grounds that there must be some connection between those whom Dante calls the *tristi* or sullen and the spiritually indifferent (*anime triste*) of the vestibule of the *Inferno*. Yet the former are granted at least the dignity of damnation while the latter go mournfully sighing forever in circles, in an eternal state of alienation. The similarity is that both possess a permanent sorrow leading to a rejection of spiritual goods, but the difference seems to be between those who have made a moral choice, though an evil one, and those who have vitiated their humanity by abstaining from moral choice itself. *Acedia,* that is, may be described as a state of soul or a disposition that can lead to disengagement, cowardice, negation, or indifference on the one hand, or, on the other, may manifest itself in sullenness, that species of anger whose victims are punished with the other wrathful.

If Laura's activities are a travesty of charity, so too are Braggioni's. Hungry men constantly wait for him outside his office or accost him on the street. "He is always sympathetic," we are told. "He gives them handfuls of small coins," and beyond this, promises. He uses them ruthlessly, and he despises them. "They are stupid, they are lazy, they are treacherous, they would cut my throat for nothing," he tells Laura. When she informs him of the death of Eugenio, Braggioni says callously, "He is a fool, and his death is his own business," and again, "He is a fool and we are well rid of him." By her passiveness and self-delusion, Laura is a passive accomplice in his crimes. St. Thomas observes that sloth, though a special vice in relation to the Divine good, may also be a circumstance of all vices in relation to the specific goods of which they are the opposites (II–II, Q. 35, Art. 2, Reply to Objections). Laura admits to herself that she may be as incomplete as Braggioni, but their conditions of incompleteness are different; they have their own distinct kinds of damnation.

Perhaps all the major spiritual differences between

them can be traced to one cause—that Laura, the idealist, feels deep attachment only to abstract principles, but none to any living thing, whereas Braggioni has no principles save that of expediency, but is possessed of a deep and passionate love. That this love is directed toward himself accounts for the fact that, far from the Pauline "vessel of abstract virtues," he is in fact a vessel of all the deadly sins (cf. II Tim.ii.21). The main details in his first appearance confirm him as one of the wrathful. He is devoted to destruction, telling Laura with some disappointment that he had once "dreamed of destroying this city, in case it offered resistance to General Ortiz, but it fell into his hands like an overripe pear." As a professional revolutionary, he is a "stirrer-up of strife" like the figure of Ira in *Piers Plowman* and might belong in the ninth bolgia of the eighth circle of Dante's *Inferno* with the "sowers of discord." Even his softer activities are portrayed in combative terms. His amours are vengeful. "A thousand women have paid for that," he says, referring to his early humiliation by a girl, and when he wishes to put an end to his music for the evening he "curves his swollen fingers around the throat of the guitar and softly smothers the music out of it." Indeed, Braggioni possesses the characteristics of all the kinds of the wrathful. He has an abiding, sullen melancholy within like St. Thomas's *amari*. Like the *acuti,* he is quick to anger, "sensitive to slights." And finally, like the *difficiles* (also known as the *graves*), he is vindictive: he is "cruel to everyone" and it is "dangerous to offend him."

In addition to wrath, Braggioni is guilty of pride and envy, the three sins in Dante's scheme of the *Purgatory* that are caused by love of the wrong objects. Of these, pride or excessive love of self, the sin of Lucifer, is primary. Braggioni is vain and sensitive because of the "vast cureless wound of his self-esteem." Like Milton's Satan, he is an effective leader because he "loves himself with such tenderness and amplitude and eternal charity that his followers . . . warm themselves in the reflected glow" and convince themselves of his nobility. His likeness to Lucifer the arch-rebel is further borne out not only by the repeated references to his being a revolutionist, but also by inversion through the many parodic details showing him as a secular Christ.

He is of vaguely foreign extraction, his father and his

name having come from another country. He is a "world-saviour" whose "skin has been punctured in honorable war-fare," but "he will never die of it." He is a "professional lover of humanity . . . wounded by life." In the first paragraph of the story when Laura returns to her home, her maid says with "a glance toward the upper room, 'He waits.'" He tells his follow-ers that "they are closer to him than his own brothers, without them he can do nothing." (cf. John, v.19 & 30, viii.28, & xv.5). He urges them to be "on the watch" (for spies) and holds forth promises of a bright future—"until tomorrow, comrade!" He is obsessed by his apocalyptic vision of the destruction of the existing world, expressed in the vivid language of eschatology. He joyously imagines everything "hurled skyward and dis-tributed, cast down again clean as rain, without separate identity . . . no one shall be left alive except the elect spirits destined to procreate a new world cleansed of cruelty and in-justice, ruled by benevolent anarchy." Finally, there is the re-union with his wife, the ceremony of her washing his feet, and their communion of weeping.

Equally Satanic is the motivation of envy, and again the author has taken pains to establish the deep-rootedness of this vice in Braggioni. Although a revolutionist dedicated to that abolition of class distinctions, he boasts of his Jockey Club perfume "imported from New York" and he is proud of his "expensive garments" tricked out with diamonds and silver ornaments. These, like his conquests of women, and like the very fat that encases him, are the satisfactions of an envy traceable to his impoverished youth when "he was so scrawny all his bones showed under his thin cotton clothing . . . and he could never find enough to eat anywhere, anywhere!" All in all, Braggioni is well endowed with the attributes of the sins of malice (Dante's *malizia* comprising all the sins of violence and fraud in the *Inferno*): "He has the malice, the cleverness, the wickedness, the sharpness of wit, the hardness of heart, stipulated for loving the world profitably."

But Porter has not neglected to suggest all the possibili-ties of wickedness in her description of Braggioni, for he is equally devoted to the "natural" sins categorized in the *In-ferno* as those of incontinence and in the *Purgatory* as those of excessive attachment to secondary goods—namely, glut-tony, avarice, and lust. His gluttony is seen in his "suety smile," his "gluttonous bulk," his oily, balloon cheeks, his "paunch between his spread knees," and his fat legs over the tops of his glossy yellow shoes swelling "with ominous ripeness." His lustfulness is evident from his designs on Laura, his boasting of his thousand conquests, and his remark that "one woman is really as good as another for me in the dark. I prefer them all." Although he is apparently not avaricious in the common sense of stinginess, he gives his poor fellows only "small coins from his own pockets" while indulging himself in every luxury; theologically, his excessive preoccupation with material goods and his desire for more of them than is necessary are the marks of avarice. "He is not rich, not in money," he tells Laura, "but in power, and this power brings with it the blameless ownership of things, and the right to indulge his love of small luxuries," such as his expensive clothes, his hired automobile, his soft bed, and his imported perfume.

Finally, there is the intermediate sin of sloth. Neither Braggioni nor Laura is guilty of that common slothfulness in the active life know as laziness (*pigritia*), for both are energetic workers in the cause. But in keeping with the general scheme of Braggioni's being perceived as a vessel of all the abstract vices, we are told of his enjoying "plenty of sleep in a soft bed beside a wife who dares not disturb him" and of his sitting "pampering his bones in easy billows of fat."

For Braggioni the sinner, there is some consolation because while everything disappoints him in the end, he at least enjoys the pleasures of his vices, revels in his power over others, and enjoys the possessions of the goods of this world. At the end of the story he is left with his wife enjoying a communion which, if it is a travesty of Christian communion, is at any rate consummated as they blend their tears, in contrast to the aborted communion in the immediately ensuing scene of Laura's dream. In the language applied by T. S. Eliot to Baudelaire, Braggioni is man enough to be damned (*Selected Essays*, 380), perhaps corresponding to the "lost violent souls" of Eliot's poem "The Hollow Men."

For Laura, on the other hand, there is no consolation. She is un-evil, but also un-good. Her children love her, but she cannot love them back. She is loved and desired by men, but can feel nothing for them. Her specific failures as a woman pre-figure her general failure as a human being. When she tries to pray, her lips, like those of Eliot's hollow men, can only "form prayers to broken stone." She continues to work for a revolutionary cause in which she no longer believes because she lacks the energy of spirit to break away. She is neat and fastidious, intelligent, intermittently perceptive, and hopelessly lost, frightened of both life and death. In spite of the likeness between her and Braggioni, which he insists upon and which she partly acknowledges, the final sense of contrast is underscored by the ironic juxtaposition of the highly colored picture of Braggioni to the overall grayness with which Laura is portrayed.

IV

> Through me lies the way to the dolorous city . . .
> Abandon all hope, you who enter.
> (*Inferno* iii. 1–9)

Not only the characters but the atmosphere of the story is saturated with the representation of the feeling most characteristic of damnation: despair. The abandonment of hope enjoined upon the damned in the legend carved upon the gate of Dante's hell may be taken as more of a description of the state of damnation than as an imperative. As St. Isidore put it in a passage cited by Aquinas, "To despair is to fall into hell" (II–II, Q. 20, Art. 3, & cf. Q. 20, Art. 4). Dante himself, as the pilgrim spirit in his poem, although he is under special divine protection, is nevertheless forbidden to gaze upon Medusa (generally understood to represent despair), the sight of whom turns men to stone. There is no special place set aside for the hopeless in hell, since an eternity of waiting without hope is precisely what hell is, a hell shared by all the damned regardless of their special sins or punishments. Even the virtuous pagans in Limbo, who suffer no special pains, are condemned to exist for eternity, as they had lived in this world, outside the pale of hope.

The fetid atmosphere of despair, of waiting without hope, permeates the whole story of "Flowering Judas." The political prisoners "of her own political faith" whom Laura visits in their cells complain that "time doesn't pass in this infernal hole." These outcast souls frequently "lose all patience and all faith" and curse their friends on the outside for not coming to their rescue, but these friends are generally little better off. They "dare not set foot in the prison for fear of disappearing into the cells kept empty for them," like the place in Dante's hell reserved for Pope Boniface VIII. Laura's errands of mercy to the prison are linked with her errands to "men hiding . . . in back streets in mildewed houses, where they sit in tumbled beds and talk bitterly." Like the damned, all are waiting, fearing, cursing, in the dark, their hopes constantly dimmed by anger and fear.

To the extent that the outcasts have any hope or faith, it is in Braggioni, whose favor "is their disputed territory." But this false saviour cynically submits them to at least purgatorial punishment. "Let them sweat a little," he says. "The next time they will be more careful." If one of them is in real danger, Laura will enter his hovel in the darkness with money and the message—and it seems impossible to overlook the sardonic pun on *Vera Cruz* (True Cross)—"Go to Vera Cruz and wait."

Laura herself both dreams and lives out a nightmare of paralysis. She too waits in dread without hope among people who "cannot understand why she is in Mexico." Like a person in a nightmare, she feels the urgent need to escape but cannot. When Braggioni, the flesh in which her revolutionary ideals have been incarnated, leaves the room, she thinks she is free—"I must run while there is time." But she does not go. With the outcasts whom she visits (as with many of the damned souls in Dante), Laura shares an intense preoccupation with time, perhaps representing all that is arbitrary in human relationships. Her body, as she prepares for sleep, does not respond to the natural rhythm. Instead, like the prisoners, she must remind herself that it is time to sleep. "Numbers tick in her brain like little clocks, soundless doors close of themselves around her" as she enters, in sleep, her own private nightmare hell.

To the many examples of theological and eschatological diction already cited many more could be added, such as Laura's private rejection of machine-made lace as a "heresy" against the religion of "her special group" who believe that "the machine is sacred, and will be the salvation of the workers." Words like "faith," "charity," "love," "patience," and "forgive" are liberally distributed through the text. The word "hope," however, does not appear, perhaps replaced by Laura's "uneasy premonitions," "disillusions," and "sense of danger."

There are also more apparent allusions to Dante than those already mentioned. Laura, for example, knowing "what Braggioni would offer her" and determined to resist, "sits in her deep chair with an open book on her knees," a picture reminiscent through ironic reversal of Francesca da Rimini whose book, instead of protecting her, has betrayed her into lust. Most striking is the pit that Laura fears to visit in her dream when Eugenio, calling her "Murderer," commands her to "follow me." "I will show you a new country," he says, with an invitation similar to that of Charon addressing the souls of the damned. The landscape through which Eugenio takes her in successive downward steps is reminiscent of the steps of hell, as she passes "the rocky ledge of a cliff and then to the jagged wave of a sea that was not water but a desert of crumbling stone." Rejecting with a cry of "No!" the recognition of evil that Eugenio attempts to force upon her, she "awoke trembling, and was afraid to sleep again," another reversal of the situation in the *Inferno* wherein Dante, trusting his guide, falls "like one overcome by sleep."

Even the colors of the story (and it is, in a quite literal sense, a very colorful story) seem to form theological patterns. The main color impression of the story derives from the title itself. No one who has ever seen the judas tree (redbud) in bloom can forget the peculiar intensity of its scarlet-to-purple flowers from which, by association with the red hair of the arch-betrayer, the tree takes its name. There is such a tree in Laura's garden, and it appears twice in the story, but never in full daylight (the *Inferno* too is a place of darkness). On the first occasion it is seen by moonlight; no stars, symbols of divine light in Dante, are mentioned. Its "scarlet blossoms" are dyed "full purple" by the darkness. Purple, the imperial color, is the prevailing color associated with Braggioni and his "lavender collar," "purple necktie," and "mauve silk hose." Thus, his link to the judas tree as the betrayer of his followers and of Laura's illusions is reinforced by the color conversion of scarlet, the theological color of charity or love, to purple, the color of empire.

The second appearance of the tree is in Laura's dream,

where it serves first as one of the steps of her downward journey, then as the supplier of the "warm bleeding flowers" which Eugenio feeds her, and finally it becomes Eugenio himself. The blossoms are now their true color of blood, but it is the blood of betrayal rather than of forgiveness in this parody of the last supper: "Murderer! said Eugenio, and Cannibal! This is my body and my blood."

Other colors in the story bring out still further theological parallels. All the colors of Laura's garden by moonlight are distortions of the colors of the theological virtues of faith, hope, and love, just as the virtues themselves appear in the story only in perverted forms. The bright white radiance of faith (sun and stars in Dante) becomes a dim replica of itself as "the moonlight spread a wash of gauzy silver over the clear spaces of the garden." The normally predominant color of a garden, green, the color of hope and also of life and carnality, is obscured by the darkness and shadows into cobalt blue, in keeping with the general absence of hope in the story. (The color green is mentioned once in the story, when Braggioni, in his song, inexplicably changes Laura's eyes from their true gray to green.) Braggioni's own "tawny yellow cat's eyes," "glossy yellow shoes," and "kinky yellow hair" suggest the leopard in Dante's *Inferno*, variously interpreted as representing lust, all the sins of incontinence, or fraud, any of which could apply to Braggioni. Finally, it is significant that when the enamored boy for whom Laura can feel nothing is singing under her window, "the names of the colors repeated themselves automatically in her mind, while she watched not the boy, but his shadow."

One last theological symbol, and perhaps the most confusing one, is the figure (he is far too shadowy to be called a character) of Eugenio. In a widely read interpretation, Ray B. West sees him as another Christ-symbol, but he accepts Eugenio at face value, basing his argument upon the meaning of the name "Eugenio"—well born—and upon his allegedly Christ-like behavior in surrendering himself up to death by means of the narcotics brought by Laura, the Juda. This, however, is an unlikely interpretation. There is nothing further in the story to indicate how Eugenio might in any way be a means of salvation, whether secular or theological. He is far too slender a figure in the story to carry such a weight, and when we add the few details about him that are given, such an interpretation becomes even more unlikely.

Eugenio's death was not a martyrdom for a cause, but a suicide brought on by boredom and despair. In Laura's dream he offers himself as the way to death, not to life: "Where are you taking me? she said. . . . To death, . . . said Eugenio." When he gives her the flowers, Laura sees "that his hand was fleshless, a cluster of small white petrified branches." Instead of the Light shining in the darkness, Laura perceives that "his eye sockets were without light."

Finally, Eugenio's metamorphosis into the tree, an image of damnation taken from Dante's forest of the suicides (*Inferno* xiii), suggests that he is to be taken parodically as much as Braggioni himself. His betrayal of life through suicide is but a more violent version of Laura's negation of life through spiritual sloth. This would seem to be the true meaning of the infernal communion between them in Laura's dream, when Eugenio says "in a voice of pity, take and eat: . . . This is my body and my blood." Although he uses the language of Jesus, his point is to confirm her a member of the damned. Eugenio cannot be taken seriously as a Christ figure, other than parodically, since he is primarily associated with despair, death, damnation, and not at all (except through reversal) with salvation.

V

> As he our darkness, cannot we his Light
> Imitate when we please?
> —*Paradise Lost* ii. 269–270

The modest conclusion to which we may come, then, is not that Porter has a positive religious message to transmit, but that, as a chronicler of the desiccation of the soul of Western humankind in our time, she found in traditional Catholic religious thought and in Dante's poetry a valid source of language and images for dealing, intensely but obliquely, with various states of spiritual vacuity and decay. It is not necessary to assume, of course, that Porter immersed herself in medieval theology, or even in Dante, in preparation for writing "Flowering

Judas." Her own account of the story's long, slow gestation and rapid, sudden composition contradicts such an idea. It is sufficient to note that Porter's early convent training and her acquaintance with the works of Eliot and Dante put her in a position where, possibly without full consciousness, she could draw upon deep reserves of psychological and ethical thought, imagery, and symbolism latent in the language and teachings of the Church and of the two poets.

Without direct evidence, no accumulation of detailed parallels can prove the thesis decisively, but it is striking how naturally all the details in the story reinforce the pattern described here, while the most careful search fails to yield one detail that contradicts it. Porter's extensive use of religious words and images in an explicitly "political" story need occasion no surprise if we consider the degree to which politics had become, in the earlier twentieth century, a substitute for religion while our religions were widely perceived as having failed to provide adequate solutions to the world's social and political problems. We are all familiar today with the equation of political creed and religion, and with the equations that derive from it—political leader with saviour, political devotee with member of a religious order, political deviation with heresy, and political disillusion with apostasy. These equations or metaphors have been exploited by the propagandists of such apocalyptic political movements as Nazism, Fascism, and Communism, and often by their opponents as well.

By exposing these religio-political metaphors to the light of political reality, Porter in "Flowering Judas" was able to reveal the danger latent in them. Personally, she was on record as being "opposed to every form of authoritarian, totalitarian government or religion." As for political expediency, she expressed herself unequivocally: "If you are promised something new and blissful at the mere price of present violence under a new master, first examine these terms carefully . . . If you are required to kill someone today, on the promise of a political leader that someone else shall live in peace tomorrow, believe me, you are not only a double murderer, you are a suicide too" (*The Days Before*, 128, 129).

"Flowering Judas" is a story about a young woman living in Mexico and working for the revolution during the 1920s. Disillusioned after her earlier commitment to a totalitarian political creed, she cannot bring herself to take any decisive action and tries to repress her internal conflict from consciousness. The story is, thus, one of self-delusion, as its author has said. It is also a story about *acedia* or spiritual life-in-death, as evidenced by its affinities to the poetry of T. S. Eliot's middle period ("The Waste Land," "Gerontion," and "The Hollow Men"). Laura "had religion" in childhood as a Roman Catholic and later as a devoted revolutionary. She lost her ability to believe in either faith and was consequently cut off from every possible heaven except one of private commitment and belief that she might construct, but she was unable or unwilling to undertake such a labor of construction.

Yet it would be unfair to put the entire responsibility for her plight upon Laura. Within the frame of reference of what her world could offer her, she seems to have done her best. "Now and again" she tried to derive some spiritual sustenance from the faith of her childhood by slipping (at the risk of scandal) into "some crumbling little church" and kneeling "on the chilly stone," but she could no more overlook the failure of her church to meet the social injustice of the society in which she found herself than she could overlook the vanity and cruelty of the revolutionary leaders. The "altar with its tinsel flowers and ragged brocades" and the "battered doll-shape of some male saint whose white, lace-trimmed drawers hang limply around his ankles" force themselves upon her unwilling attention. The tinsel flowers suggest a divorce from reality in contrast to the "fresh garden flowers" left on her desk each day by the adoring children in her classroom, representing immaculate love, to the "warm bleeding flowers" of her dream, representing a perversion of spiritual love, and even to the flower that she heedlessly tossed to her anonymous young suitor and that he continues to wear, "withering in his hat," representing a failure of human love.

Her religion of politics, on the other hand, offers her no closer tie with reality. The "developed sense of reality" of her comrades seems to her no more than cynicism, and Mrs. Braggioni's sense of reality, which was "beyond criticism," consists merely of her recognition and acceptance of her own enslavement. Just as the enternal basis of hell is an inversion of the unchanging bliss of heaven, so is a nightmare a horrific transformation of reality. Laura's nightmare existence is symbolized by her vision of herself sitting with Braggioni "with a bitter anxiety, as if tomorrow may not come, but time may be caught immovably in this hour, and with herself transfixed, Braggioni singing on forever and Eugenio's body not yet discovered by the guard."

And yet time does move, or at any rate it conveys the illusion of movement. The seasons pass and return in endless rhythm. But for those who are fearful of death or of life the movement itself is frightful. The time of the story is April, with May rapidly approaching (the "depraved May" of Eliot's "Gerontion"), and both the Catholics and the Socialists are making their plans for the celebration of life's renewal. For the unliving and the undead, however, April may be the "cruellest month," and the renewal of life is an agony to be shunned like death. Braggioni, apostle of death, is excited by the prospect of the approaching May-day, for he will come alive in his element of violence. He tells Laura "about the May-day disturbances coming on in Morelia, for the Catholics hold a festival in honor of the Blessed Virgin, and the Socialists celebrate their martyrs on that day. 'There will be two independent processions, starting from either end of town, and they will march until they meet, and the rest depends . . .'" Laura, on the other hand, reacts with fright and revulsion. As she looks down the barrel of the pistol she has been cleaning for Braggioni, "a long, slow faintness rises and subsides in her."

Two processions moving ineluctably toward mutual catastrophe—this is the metaphor for Laura's world. One procession seems to be grounded in a no longer viable past, putting its faith in unrealities, while the other, boasting a developed sense of reality, seems in fact to offer only death or tyranny. They divide the world of the story between them, and while each offers to the artist a vocabulary of words and images useful to set off the failures of the other, neither, in this context, seems to exist in relation to any other reality.

Here we see, behind the story of one young woman's failure, a world "heaving in the sickness of millennial change." If she were an artist, Laura might not be cut off from all life and joy if she could really love the children she teaches or could cultivate the finer shades of interpersonal relationships, the doctrine offered in many of the English novels of the earlier twentieth century. Perhaps love would offer some hope of personal redemption in the midst of chaos, as Matthew Arnold half-heartedly suggested more than a century ago in "Dover Beach." It does occur to Laura that love is indeed what survives, as she thinks of the youth who follows her, observing the convention of love "with all propriety, as though it were founded on a law of nature, which in the end it might very well prove to be." But even if possible, would such a personal salvation be enough when all around her, in the Mexico which is her Inferno, Laura sees only confusion, the confusion of "love with revolution, night with day, life with death," and beyond this nothing. Such questions are at least implicit in Laura's story, and they must be considered before she can be judged or condemned.

Because of the absence of any viable faith in "Flowering Judas," it is a portrayal of a hell without a heaven. It is perhaps in this sense that the story is a fragment, as the *Inferno* would be a fragment without the rest of the *Divine Comedy,* or the first two books of *Paradise Lost* would be a fragment without the portrayal of the two paradises of heaven and earth. This absence in no way detracts, however, from the power of the story, for its symbiosis of religious and political imagery offers a profound and moving experience of the failure of two of the great faiths of our epoch. Porter's complex, parodic symbolism of life and death, salvation and damnation, good and evil, contributes inestimably to the depth of insight offered by the story into the failure of the individual which reflects and is reflected in the "majestic and terrible failure of man in the Western world."

 Notes ■

1. *Recent Southern Fiction: A Panel Discussion,* Wesleyan College, Macon, Georgia. Quoted in "News and Ideas," *College English* 22 (1961): 521.

■ DAVID MADDEN ■

The Charged Image in Katherine Anne Porter's "Flowering Judas"

In *Writers at Work, Second Series,* the interviewer asked Katherine Anne Porter whether "Flowering Judas" began as a visual impression that grew into a narrative. "All my senses were very keen," Miss Porter replied. "Things came to me through my eyes, through all my pores. Everything hit me at once. . . ." Without words or images, her stories began to form. Then she starts thinking "directly in words. Abstractly. Then the words transform themselves into images." [1] On several occasions Miss Porter has testified to the potency of the real-life image that generated "Flowering Judas."

She chose this story for inclusion in an anthology called *This Is My Best* (1942). Commenting on the story at that time, she said: "All the characters and episodes are based on real persons and events, but naturally, as my memory worked upon them and time passed, all assumed different shapes and colors, formed gradually around a central idea, that of self-delusion. . . ." [2] In the *Paris Review* interview some twenty years later, she elaborated:

> That story had been on my mind for years, growing out of this one little thing that happened in Mexico. . . . Something I saw as I passed a window one evening. A girl I knew had asked me to come and sit with her, because a man was coming to see her, and she was a little afraid of him. And as I went through the courtyard, past the flowering judas tree, I glanced in the window and there she was sitting with an open book

From *Studies in Short Fiction* 7 (1970): 277–289.

on her lap, and there was this great big fat man sitting beside her. Now Mary and I were friends, both American girls living in this revolutionary situation. She was teaching at an Indian school, and I was teaching dancing at a girls' technical school in Mexico City. And we were having a very strange time of it (1965).

• • •

I had a brief glimpse of her sitting with an open book in her lap, but not reading, with a fixed look of pained melancholy and confusion in her face. The fat man I call Braggioni was playing the guitar and singing to her [1942].

• • •

And when I looked through that window that evening, I saw something in Mary's face, something in her pose, something in the whole situation, that set up a commotion in my mind [1965].

• • •

In that glimpse, no more than a flash, I thought I understood, or perceived, for the first time, the desperate complications of her mind and feelings, and I knew a story; perhaps not her true story, not even the real story of the whole situation, but all the same a story that seemed symbolic truth to me. If I had not seen her face at that very moment, I should never have written just this story because I should not have known it to write [1942].

• • •

Because until that moment I hadn't really understood that she was not able to take care of herself, because she was not able to face her own nature and was afraid of everything. I don't know why I saw it. I don't believe in intuition. When you get sudden flashes of perception, it is just the brain working faster than usual. But you've been getting ready to know it for a long time, and when it comes, you feel you've known it always [1965].

As raw material for literature, this real-life image was already, implicitly, dynamically charged with feeling and meaning. The author's physical distance from her friend that evening was an analog to the objectivity that was necessary when she transformed the real-life image into the fictive image. And out of this actual image was to grow also the structural, stylistic, and technical conceptions of "Flowering Judas," a created, transcendent image with an organic life of its own. This story is one of the most lucid exemplifications I know of what Croce calls "the aesthetic image," compounded of "a tissue of images," and of what I call *the charged image*. Ezra Pound's definition of great literature as "language charged with meaning to the utmost possible degree" (to "meaning" I would add the word "feeling") suggests the source of power in "Flowering Judas." Before I feel out the anatomy of this charged image, I want to quote Miss Porter again.

Soon after *Flowering Judas*, her first book of stories, was published in 1930, Miss Porter wrote to a friend:

> I can't tell you what gives true intensity, but I know it when I find it, even in my own work. . . . It is not a matter of how you feel at any one moment, certainly not at the moment of writing. A calculated coldness is the best mood for that most often. Feeling is more than a mood; it is a whole way of being; it is the nature you're born with, you cannot invent it. The question is how to convey a sense of whatever is there, as feeling, within you, to the reader; and that is a problem of technical expertness.[3]

Mr. Hagopian's response to Miss Porter's statement reflects my own conviction: "Thus, from the beginning, Miss Porter knew what she was doing—embodying the *true intensity* of experience into literary form with *technical expertness*." Mark Schorer, writing about technique in general, describes what Miss Porter does most brilliantly in "Flowering Judas": "When we speak of technique, then, we speak of nearly everything. For technique is the means by which the writer's experience, which is his subject matter, compels him to attend to it; technique is the only means he has of discovering, exploring, developing his subject, of conveying its meaning, and, finally, of evaluating it." Technique "objectifies the materials of art." The forms of the finest works of fiction, Schorer argues, are "exactly equivalent with their subjects," and "the evaluation of their subjects exists in their styles." He cites Miss Porter's work as exemplary. "The cultivated sensuosity" of Miss Porter's style has not only "charm in itself" but "esthetic value . . .

its values lie in the subtle means by which sensuous details become symbols, and in the way the symbols provide a network which is the story, and which at the same time provides the writer and us with a refined moral insight by means of which to test it.[4] Some readers may cite Miss Porter's phrase "a calculated coldness" to explain the coldness her technique and her sensibility instill in some of her stories. But that phrase and her comments in *Writers at Work* suggest her attitude about technique as a means of discovery; although she testifies that she knew the ending of "Flowering Judas" before she began to write (as she *usually* knows the ending before she begins to write a story), the powerful final stroke came unconsciously (but was made possible, most probably, by her habitual consciousness of technique). "I knew that the vengeful spirit was going to come in a dream to tow her away into death, but I didn't know until I'd written it that she was going to wake up saying, 'No!' and be afraid to sleep again." Although, as friends and critics have observed, one must regard Miss Porter's comments on her own work with almost the same caution with which one regards Faulkner's self-scrutiny, it is no contradiction of our image of Miss Porter as a conscious craftsman that she claims to write her stories in single spurts of energy. "I always write a story in one sitting. I started 'Flowering Judas' at seven p.m. and at one-thirty I was standing on a snowy windy corner putting it in the mailbox" (*Writers at Work*). Miss Porter glimpsed a girl and a man through a window in Mexico City and two years later, in a few hours in Brooklyn, recaptured and transformed that image into a work of art.

In her introduction to *The Selected Short Stories of Eudora Welty* (1954), Miss Porter describes the kind of story she prefers: one in which "external act and the internal voiceless life of the human imagination almost meet and mingle on the mysterious threshold between dream and waking, one reality refusing to admit or confirm the other, yet both conspiring toward the same end."[5] Magalaner and Volpe declare that "Flowering Judas" is "from the first word of the title to the last word of the text" a model of that kind of story. They go on to say that it "is a sensitive and discerning philosophical statement of human relationships, made universal by the mythic elements which intrude as early as the hint in the title." But more than that, it is a remarkable aesthetic achievement to which we may return again and again, just as we return to Keats's "Ode on a Grecian Urn"; for long after we have absorbed its universal philosophical and psychological truths, "Flowering Judas" remains a "thing of beauty," a "joy forever," embodying Keats's declaration that "Beauty is truth, truth beauty."

In some ways "Flowering Judas" resembles literary form less than it resembles dance, mother of all the arts, especially of poetry and of the most contemporary of the arts—cinema (I use these analogies simply for their suggestiveness). The dynamic imagery of dance, the compression and the expressive juxtapositions of poetry, and the montage effects of Eisenstein's cinema are transmuted by Miss Porter, unconsciously, I imagine, into fictive techniques that produce what interests and moves me most in this story—the charged image. The omniscient author's psychological analysis of and philosophical reflections about Laura's predicament and the self-delusory processes that follow from her predicament are everywhere in the story, suffusing the very style that creates the tissue of images. But overwhelming her own overt interpretations when they threaten to intimidate the life of the story, the images embody Miss Porter's meaning with expressive vitality; ultimately, of course, this vitality cannot be separated from the vitality of Miss Porter's meditations about Laura. The story exfoliates from a tight intermingling of showing and telling. And that story, were it not for the author's technique of dramatically juxtaposing tableaux, is so rich and multifaceted as to require the scope of a novel.

As the elements of Laura's exterior and interior worlds intermingle, they cohere in a developing pattern of images which expands from the charged image that inspired Miss Porter in life and that she sets forth in the beginning of her fiction:

> Braggioni sits heaped upon the edge of a straight-backed chair much too small for him, and sings to Laura in a furry, mournful voice. Laura has begun to find reasons for avoiding her own house until the latest possible moment, for Braggioni is there almost every night. No matter how late she is, he will be sitting there with a surly, waiting expression, pulling at his

kinky yellow hair, thumbing the strings of his guitar, snarling a tune under his breath. Lupe the Indian maid meets Laura at the door, and says with a flicker of a glance towards the upper room, "He waits."

This central, most potent image is the hub, and all other images spoke out from it, and the author's meditating voice is the rim, and (to complete the metaphor) the reader's active participation is the energy that makes the wheel turn. Paralyzed, Laura is locked into this image, as though in a small box stage set, and we see her at a distance, as though through the original real-life window. With each image that Miss Porter shows us, we feel that Laura is withdrawing more and more deeply into herself, that her will is becoming more and more paralyzed. The controlling image (Laura and Braggioni sitting opposite each other by the table) is a simplified visual and thematic expression of the entire story; this image recurs at strategic points in the pattern, creating that sense of simultaneity that makes a work of art cohere and seem inevitable. Laura's posture varies only slightly; and though Braggioni is singing and playing his guitar, the tableau virtually does not move—it vibrates from within, sending its electrical charge in a radial fashion out into the other images connected to it.

In 1961 at Centre College in Kentucky, I discussed "Flowering Judas" with my two classes of freshman students. Mystification over my charged-image concept only compounded their boredom with the story itself. To enable them to see Miss Porter's story, and my point, more clearly, I arranged a demonstration with the Drama Department. Using multi-level space staging and lighting as a means of isolating one acting area, one scene, from another, we mounted a series of tableaux in pantomime, while a young woman read the story over a public address system. The images enacted were these (following the sequence in the story):

Laura and Braggioni sit opposite each other by the table.

In the first image that is juxtaposed, montage-fashion, to this hub image, we see Laura sitting in church.

Cut to Braggioni at the table in Laura's house again, singing, playing the guitar.

Fade to Laura in the classroom with Indian children.

Fade to a composite image: Laura at a union meeting; Laura visiting prisoners in cells; Laura meeting men in dark doorways with messages; Laura meeting with Polish and Roumanian agitators in cafés.

Fade to another composite image: Laura riding horseback with the Captain; Laura and the Captain at a table in a restaurant; Laura in the classroom responding to a floral design and a message of affection to her drawn on the blackboard; Laura at her window responding to the youth who serenades her.

Fade to another composite: Laura and the children again; Laura at the doors of fugitives again.

Cut to Laura and Braggioni at the table again; he talks of love; her response is negative. Superimposed image of Braggioni in the streets.

Fade to a composite: Braggioni's wife weeping on the floor in her room; Eugenio's body lying on the floor of his cell.

Cut to Laura with Braggioni again; she cleans his pistols; Braggioni puts his gun belt on.

Fade to Laura in the street on errands again, meeting strange faces.

Fade to a composite: Braggioni and his wife; she washes his feet; they eat; they lie in bed together.

Cut to composite image: Laura in white in bed; Laura at dark doors; Laura with children in classroom; Laura with prisoners.

Fade to Laura with Eugenio in a nightmare, as he leads her away, offering her the blossoms of the Judas tree to eat.

Cut to Laura awake, crying No! She is afraid to sleep again.

To this day, students tell me that this dramatic enactment of the story's charged image structure was one of the most electrifying theatrical experiences they have ever had. Re-reading the story itself, they were able to come closer to the kind of experiences the story offers readers who are more aesthetically responsive.

Miss Porter's technique of creating a dynamic interplay among images that are strategically spaced in an unfolding pattern is appropriate for the rendering of Laura's state of mind—self-delusion producing paralysis of will. Not only does she move very little in the recurrent scene set in the present, but her recent, habitual past life as well is presented in terms of static images. The reader feels the tension between these static images and Laura's impulse within the images to flee. From a positive standpoint, the static quality of the pictures is expressive of Laura's desire for stasis. The energy of the story is transmitted in the kinetic juxtaposition of one charged image to another. A few similes may make my simple point even clearer: reading the story is like watching a single photograph, simple in outline but rich in detail, yield more and more auxiliary images each time it is redeveloped and enlarged (I am thinking of the experience the photographer has in the movie *Blow-Up*); or the images are superimposed, causing a cumulative density of texture; or reading the story is like watching a cubist painting being painted, from the first stroke, the title, to the last word, No.

The contrast between the static quality of the images and the immediacy of the historical present tense generates a tension that enhances the effect of Miss Porter's basic image technique. She declares that not until someone asked her why she used it did she realize she had employed the historical present tense. In any case, it is clear that the present tense keeps the images themselves alive while they portend the incipient moribundity of Laura, the character who is at the center of each (even when, in the scene in Braggioni's hotel room, she isn't physically present). Miss Porter's technique resembles the early montage techniques of the European movies of the late Twenties and anticipates cinematic methods used by Resnais in *Hiroshima, Mon Amour* and *Last Year at Marienbad*. She shows us one scene, stops the camera, goes on to another scene, goes back to an earlier scene, holds, then goes further back to an even earlier scene, then leaps far ahead. But the image technique is also similar to one used long before the birth of the cinema—Spenser's tableau juxtapositions in *The Faerie Queen*.

Laura has just come from the prison and "is waiting for tomorrow with a bitter anxiety. . . . but time may be caught immovably in this hour, with herself transfixed, Braggioni singing on forever, and Eugenio's body not yet discovered by the guard." The result of Miss Porter's charged image technique is that the reader is left with this timeless image of Laura sitting opposite Braggioni at the table, transfixed in fear and accidie,[6] all the other images clustered around her like spokes in a hub. Laura's one act in the present tense of the story comes toward the end: "The presence of death in the room makes her bold," so she "holds up the [gun] belt to him: 'Put that on, and go kill somebody in Morelia, and you will be happier!'" This is a futile gesture. In numerous little ways, Laura herself, we have seen, has already killed various kinds of generous human impulses toward love, including Braggioni's. So at this point, the recurrent static picture at the hub of all the other images moves, but to no purpose: Braggioni leaves, Laura goes to sleep.

Along with her use of present tense, Miss Porter's frequent use of questions—"Where could she go?"—is another technique for enlivening her overt thematicizing and the progression of static images. And the routineness of Laura's life is another element that makes Miss Porter's technique of repeating the same images in a pattern effective.

Laura was dehumanized herself by encasing herself "in a set of principles derived from early training, leaving no detail of gesture or of personal taste untouched." Miss Porter's attitude toward people like Laura is suggested in her comment on a certain kind of writer: "By accepting any system and shaping his mind and work to that mold, the artist dehumanizes himself, unfits himself for the practice of any art" (quoted in Magalaner, p. 127). Braggioni tells Laura that they are more alike than she realizes; she sees the possibility of her being as "corrupt, in another way, as Braggioni . . . as callous, as incomplete," but rather than do something about these faults, she prefers "any kind of death." Figuratively, Laura and Braggioni reveal two perspectives on a single person; each exhibits aspects of the other. They also contrast with each other. But finally, Laura's personality embodies many aspects of Braggioni's, carrying them to a negative extreme. It is appropriate, then, that Miss Porter employs a modified omniscient point of view, favoring Laura, but shifting, strategically, to Braggioni near the end.

Braggioni, "a professional lover of humanity," who began as a "hungry world-savior," but who will never die of this love (one of many suggestions that he is a false Christ), tells Laura his true feelings about the common men who follow him: any of them might easily turn Judas (as, in spirit, Laura already has). In many instances, Laura is a Magdalene to one man, a false Magdalene or a Judas to others. Loyalty to one group necessitates Laura's betrayal of trust in other groups; thus "she borrows money from the Roumanian agitator to give to his bitter enemy the Polish agitator"; through her, Braggioni *uses* these people.

"Flowering Judas" delineates a maze of ambiguity of roles, beginning with Laura and Braggioni, going on down to the minor characters. Everyone seems to be both a savior and a Judas to everyone else. Braggioni is both a false and, in a purely human way of course, a real Christ to various people; but he is also a Judas. So is Laura both secular savior and betrayer of the same people. The author conceives of these complex savior-Judas relationships paradoxically and ironically and enhances them with a controlled atmosphere of ambiguity; this nexus of savior-Jesus analogies extends from the inner psychological realm of Laura and Braggioni out into the public realm and up to a symbolic level. Many kinds of service and betrayal are depicted and implied in the story; but Laura, by denying sex, love, meaningful purpose, and action, inclines too far toward betrayal, as the climactic nightmare scene stresses.

Miss Porter shifts scene and point of view deliberately for a dramatic contrast to Laura. Returning to his wife, who is still weeping, Braggioni is glad to be back in a familiar place where the smells are good and his wife does not reproach him, but offers to wash his feet (she is a genuine Magdalene to his Christ-role). We see that Braggioni is in many ways a more creative person than Laura. Out of remorse, he weeps, saying, "Ah, yes, I am hungry, I am tired, let us eat something together." His supper with his wife contrasts with Laura's devouring of the Judas flowers. His wife asks his forgiveness for failing to be sufficient to all his needs, and her tears refresh him—she weeps *for* him as well as because of him. At least with one other person, Braggioni experiences a rich sexual and affectionate relationship. He is lonely, soft, guilt-ridden, we see now, though we've sensed this all along; but because of his external public role and because of her rigid demeanor, Braggioni and Laura were unable to meet. Rilke says that "love consists in this, that two solitudes protect, and touch and greet each other." If nothing more, Braggioni and his wife experience this touching of solitudes.

Now Miss Porter shifts point of view back to Laura as she "takes off her serge dress and puts on a white linen night-gown and goes to bed." Her virginal uniform of white mocks her sterility. She thinks of her children as prisoners who bring their "jailor" flowers. Numbers tick in her brain, turning her mind into a clock, a machine. Within her own solitude of mind and flesh, Laura cries out in anguish that "it is monstrous to confuse love with revolution, night with day, life with death," and invokes Eugenio's spirit "—ah, Eugenio!"

The midnight bell seems to be a signal she can't understand. Miss Porter handles the intermingling of interior and exterior worlds so adroitly that the dream passage comes with a controlled abruptness, and the change in tone does not jar, but seems inevitable. Without warning the reader, Miss Porter has Eugenio speak to Laura—without quotation marks, for his voice is pure expression, like an object. Echoing Christ's command to his followers, he tells Laura to get up and follow him. He asks her why she is in this strange house (in Mexico, in the world, in her own mind; one thinks of Lucifer's "The mind is its own place, and in itself/Can make a Heav'n of Hell, a Hell of Heav'n."). Here Miss Porter, though she is describing a dream that is happening now, shifts into the past tense to enhance our feeling that Laura's life, insofar as its capacity for responding to possibilities, is over, whether literally she dies soon after the story ends or not.

Eugenio calls Laura a murderer (she is *his* Judas, but the charge covers all her crimes of the body, the mind, and the spirit, for they affect *other* bodies, minds, and spirits, including his own.) But even to his offer to take her to a new country, death, Laura says, "No," fearing anything more than the fear to which she has grown accustomed and from which she is unable to imagine a separate identity for herself.

Miss Porter gives the reader a sense of the fluid, surre-alistic changes of the nightmare landscape as Laura clings to the "stair rail, and then to the topmost branch of the Judas tree that bent down slowly and set her upon the earth, and then to the rocky ledge of a cliff, and then to the jagged wave of a sea that was not water but a desert of crumbling stone."

All this suggests again Eliot's mental-physical Waste Land, and "The Love Song of J. Alfred Prufrock," and, as one critic has pointed out, "Gerontion," as well.

The ambiguous title of the story interprets all its images. The Judas tree gets its name from the belief that from such a tree Judas hanged himself. Abundant purple flowers appear in the spring before the leaves. A certain elder is called a Judas tree because it bears "Jew's ear," an edible, cup-shaped flower, resembling an ear, which is cherished as a medicine. So the tree itself and Miss Porter's title ultimately have both positive and negative connotations, and the story depicts in its charged images the gestures of both betrayers and betrayed; the reader feels his way through an ambiguity that deliberately makes it difficult to distinguish with any final clarity one from the other. Thus, Eugenio, who has qualities of Christ, as one betrayed offers *Judas* flowers to Laura, the betrayer; and thus, in eating the body of Christ cannibalistically she is also eating the body of Judas, for Eugenio, too, is a kind of Judas, betraying Laura. But the "flowering Judas" is Laura.

Eugenio offers her the flowers of the Judas tree, and as she devours them, he calls her "Murderer!" and "Cannibal!" "This is my body and my blood. Laura cried No! and at the sound of her own voice, she awoke trembling, and was afraid to sleep again." She wakes, but not to enlightenment (although one may argue that it is perhaps enlightenment that makes her afraid to sleep again), for the dominating idea in her life, as in the nightmare, is denial, and with this No, Miss Porter appropriately ends the story. By now the No (in contrast to the Yes with which Molly Bloom ends *Ulysses*) is both a strong auditory image and an object. Just as Eugenio's eyes, unlike Christ's, do not bring light, the dream does not result in self-revelation for Laura, and her self-delusion persists at the end, along with the paralysis of her will (reminiscent of Gabriel Conroy's predicament at the end of "The Dead," a story that concludes with a similar elegiac vision). When we discover Laura sitting at the table in the initial, persistent charged image, she has already lost in her conflict between ideal aspiration and actuality. What self-knowledge she has she fails to employ in an act of self-discovery.

While "Flowering Judas" is not concerned with religion in itself, suggestive religious terms and motifs recur throughout the story. The images are almost like black parodies of religious icons or such tapestries as the Bayeux, or scenes in church panel paintings, frescoes, and mosaics (scenes of worship, charity, love, and betrayal). Miss Porter's frequent use of paradox in style and characterization suggests her purpose in employing religious motifs—as analogies to patterns of human behavior and relationships on secular levels.

While politics is closer than religion to Miss Porter's concern with her characters as people alive or dying in the secular world, politics, too, functions almost expressionistically. Braggioni tells Laura about the May-day disturbances soon to occur. On the same day on which Catholics hold a festival in honor of the Virgin (a parallel to Laura, whose virginity is neither spiritual nor quite natural), the Socialists will celebrate their martyrs, and the two processions, coming from opposite ends of town, will clash. Thus, rather neatly, Miss Porter summarizes in a composite dialogue image the two conflicting public contexts (religious and political) of Laura's private despair. There is almost no sustained dialogue in the story until this scene; the fragments of dialogue are verbal parallels to the series of charged visual images. On Laura, Braggioni's voice has the same hypnotic effect it has on crowds; and as he expresses his vision of a world completely destroyed so that a better world of "benevolent anarchy" can be built upon the ruins, Laura feels he has forgotten her as a person. He will create a physical Waste Land (an objective correlative to the spiritual Waste Land of which Laura is a major exemplification). All separate identity will vanish, and "no one shall be alive except the elect spirits destined to procreate a new world" (that excludes Laura).

Institutionalized religion and political ideals, perverted in revolution, are escapes from ordinary love. Laura refuses not only Braggioni but the Captain and the youth as lovers; more crucial to her general dilemma is her failure even in non-sexual ways, for she cannot even love the children she teaches, nor Eugenio, the man to whom she offers release from the world in which she herself must continue to suffer. Failure to distinguish illusion from reality in the conflict between ideal aspiration and brutal actuality produces Laura's self-delusion and the "No" with which she arms herself against the world. Thus, she waits in fear; a sense of overwhelming futility paralyzes her.

In preparation for the public violence that is imminent, Laura, who so intensely fears violence to herself, oils and loads Braggioni's pistols; no more grotesque half-parody of Freudian symbolism can be imagined. Laura peers down Braggioni's "pistol barrel and says nothing." The barrel's sexual connotation is reinforced by the literal lethalness of its purpose. Corresponding with this double-barreled significance Laura feels "a long, slow faintness" rising and subsiding in her, while Braggioni "curves his swollen fingers around the throat of the guitar and softly smothers the music out of it." This juxtaposition is the most powerful of several in which Miss Porter makes the guitar an analogy to Laura's body.

A psychological examination of Laura will reveal the organic unity of the story more closely. One may look at Laura in light of six forces that, simultaneously, dominate her life: 1) Laura's predominant state of mind is denial: No. Her general negativity as she waits in fear is the frame for everything else we discover about her. 2) she rejects sex; she evades love; she substitutes a grim charity; she radiates a deadly innocence. 3) She gives everything (though it is not enough) to revolutionary politics, while refusing social fellowship and religious transcendence. 4) She fails to distinguish between illusion and reality. 5) Denying everything, overwhelmed by a sense of futility, she waits in fear of violent death. 6) These dominant elements in the story suggest a missing element: self-realization. But the reader sees what Laura fails to see. If one examine the story from beginning to end keeping in mind the pattern of images delineated earlier, one may see how each of these aspects of Laura's psychological and physical predicament is embodies in charged images that recur and cluster. I have suggested the thematic content that Miss Porter's images embody. In his introduction to *The Nigger of the Narcissus*, Joseph Conrad said: "A work that aspires, however humbly, to the condition of art should carry its justification in every line." "Flowering Judas" realizes that aspiration to an uncommon degree.

134

☐ *Notes* ■

1. *Writers at Work: The Paris Review Interviews,* Second Series (New York: The Viking Press, 1965), 137–163.

2. *This Is My Best,* Whit Burnett, ed. (New York: The Dial Press, 1942), 539.

3. Quoted in John V. Hagopian's review of *The Collected Stories of Katherine Anne Porter* in *Studies in Short Fiction* 4, 86.

4. "Technique as Discovery," in Schorer's selected essays, *The World We Imagine* (New York, 1968), 3–23.

5. Quoted in *Twelve Short Stories,* Marvin Magalaner and Edmond L. Volpe, eds. (New York, 1961), 127–129.

6. In "Laura and the Unlit Lamp," *Studies in Short Fiction* 1, 61–63, Sister Mary Bride makes this observation; she also notes that Laura's name is ironic if we remember Petrarch's Laura.

Revolution and the Female Principle in "Flowering Judas"

"Flowering Judas" has almost always been interpreted as a story about revolution and betrayal, and any critical confusion has centered on the extent to which Laura is in fact the betrayer, the "Judas." Ray West's early analysis of Laura as betrayer because she brings no love to the revolution has been the most widely accepted interpretation for many years.[1] However, even West's theory does not answer all the important questions about the story, as M. M. Liberman, among others, has pointed out.[2] In an interview with Barbara Thompson and in Whit Burnett's *This Is My Best,* Porter identified the model for Laura as her friend Mary Doherty, who like Laura taught Indian children in Xochimilco and participated in the revolution.[3] Some critics, however, have correctly seen Laura as a combination of Mary Doherty and Porter herself and thus Laura as a somewhat autobiographical character, an embryonic version of Miranda, who first appears as a character in Porter's fiction five years after the publication of "Flowering Judas." If Laura is examined not only in the light of Porter's experiences in the Mexican revolution but also in the light of Miranda's experiences in "The Circus," "The Fig Tree," and "The Grave," Laura herself emerges as a character better understood, and the theme of betrayal in the story is more clearly defined.

From *Truth and Vision in Katherine Anne Porter's Fiction* (Athens: University of Georgia Press, 1985).

Among Porter's papers is a sketch hand-dated 1921,
preliminary to the story that became "Flowering Judas." It is
not inconsistent with her description of the genesis of the
story in her interview with Thompson and in *This Is My Best*,
and it does help illuminate the character of Laura. It is worth
examining carefully:

> Yudico cam[e] tonight bringing his guitar, and spent the
> eve[ning] singing for Mary.
>
> Mary sat in a deep chair at the end of the table, under the
> light, a little preoccupied, infallible and kindly attentive. She
> is a modern secular nun. Her mind is chaste and wise, she
> knows a great deal about life at twenty three, and is a virgin
> but faintly interested in love. She wears a rigid little uniform
> of dark blue cloth, with immaculate collars and cuffs of nar-
> row lace made by hand. There is something dishonest, she
> thinks in lace contrived by machinery. She is very poor, but
> she pays a handsome price for her good, honest lace, her one
> extravagance.
>
> Being born Catholic and Irish, her romantic sense of ad-
> venture has guided her very surely to the lower strata of revo-
> lution. Backed by a course of economics at the Rand School,
> she keeps her head cool in the midst of opera bouffe plots,
> the submerged international intrigue of her melodramatic
> associates.
>
> She had meant to organise the working women of Mexico
> into labour unions. It would all have worked beautifully if
> there had been any one else in the whole country as clear
> and straight minded as Mary. But there wasn't, and she has
> got a little new pucker of trouble between her wide set grey
> eyes, within four weeks of her arrival. She doesn't in the least
> comprehend that revolution is also a career to the half dozen
> or so initiates who are managing it, and finding herself subtly
> blocked and hindered at every turn, she set it down to her
> own lack of understanding of the special problems of la-
> bour in Mexico. . . . She has been bludgeoned into a certain
> watchful acquiescence by that phrase. So that now she has
> the look of one who expects shortly to find a simple and hon-
> est solution to a very complicated problem. She is never to
> find it.[4]

When the notes were made Porter would have been in Mexico probably less than a year, but according to published essays and her letters to friends and family, she already had lost many of her illusions. The story "Flowering Judas," completed some years later, relies upon the essential elements of the sketch, but Mary has become Laura, Yudico has become Braggioni, and it is Mrs. Braggioni who organizes the working women. In the note, Mary has been jolted into the realization that no one else in the revolution is "as clear and straight minded" as she is. And so she "has got a little new pucker of trouble between her wide set grey eyes." But she nevertheless "has the look of one who expects shortly to find a simple and honest solution to a very complicated problem." The Laura of the published story, however, is a step beyond the Mary of the sketch. She no longer expects to find a simple solution. She has glimpsed the reality and the dangers and has avoided both by withdrawing to a state of deadened feeling while simply carrying out the ritual of the revolution. "Like a good child," she "understands the rules of behavior."

Laura represents the alien who came to Mexico "uninvited" to participate in the revolution. In so doing she ostensibly had to abandon her own Catholicism and take on the "religion" of revolution because the Church was an enemy of the revolution in Mexico. One supposes that Laura has joined the revolution with the kind of fervor that shows in Porter's own early remarks about it. But now Laura has become disillusioned with the hypocrisy of the movement, even with her own participation. She goes to union meetings, takes food, cigarettes, messages, and a little money to prisoners, "smuggles letters from headquarters to men hiding from firing squads in the back streets in mildewed houses," borrows money from one agitator to give to another, and teaches English to Indian children. But Laura feels betrayed. Her idealistic view of the revolution has not been confirmed. Sometimes she wishes to run away, but she stays because "she has promised herself to this place; she can no longer imagine herself as living in another country, and there is no pleasure in remembering her life before she came here." She cannot define "the nature of this devotion, its true motives . . . its obligations."[5] Like many other outsiders who came to aid in

139

the revolution, she feels obligated to stay through to some conclusion, even in the face of disillusionment.

Braggioni is the symbol of Laura's disillusions, for she had thought of a revolutionist as "lean, animated by heroic faith, a vessel of abstract virtues," essentially a Christ figure. Braggioni's distance from this standard is implied in all the descriptions of him. The irony is established early in the story when "the Indian maid meets Laura at the door and says with a flicker of a glance towards the upper room, 'He waits.'" He who is waiting has already been described as "sitting there with a surly, waiting expression, pulling at his kinky yellow hair, . . . snarling a tune under his breath," surely not the description of a "vessel of abstract virtues." The reference to the upper room is an allusion to the place of the Last Supper, and the maid's warning, "He waits," is an allusion to Christ.[6] The story thus is framed by symbolic, if ironic, allusions to the sacred supper at which Christ and his disciples celebrate the Passover, significantly a celebration of one people's escape from bondage. It is at the Last Supper that Jesus instructs his disciples in the meaning of feet washing, that the Sacrament of Holy Communion is observed, and that Jesus predicts Judas's betrayal. Later in the story Mrs. Braggioni washes her husband's feet, Laura symbolically betrays herself, and in her dream she participates in a parody of Holy Communion.

Braggioni once had been closer to Laura's revolutionary ideal; he once at least had been lean, if not animated by heroic faith. Indeed, "once he was called Delgadito by all the girls and married women who ran after him; he was so scrawny all his bones showed under his thin cotton clothing, and he could squeeze his emptiness to the very backbone with his two hands. He was a poet and the revolution was only a dream then." He has forgotten his hunger, however, and in spite of his incompetent singing is a symbolic figurehead of the poets who write "about romance and the stars, and roses and the shadowy eyes of ladies, touching no sorrow of the human heart other than the pain of unrequited love." In fact, it was unrequited love that animated Braggioni. "When he was fifteen, he tried to drown himself because he loved a girl, his first love, and she laughed at him. 'A thousand women have paid for that.'" And so he indulges himself with food and women and nourishes his self-love. "Too many women loved him and sapped away his youth, and he could never find enough to eat anywhere, anywhere!" He has good food and abundant drink . . . and enjoys plenty of sleep in a soft bed beside a wife who dares not disturb him; and he sits pampering his bones in easy billows of fat." He tells Laura, "One woman is really as good as another for me, in the dark. I prefer then all." He perfumes his hair with imported Jockey Club.

The same ideal motivates others in the story who mirror Braggioni's misplaced fervor. For example, the shock-haired youth who serenades Laura is an organizer of the Typographers Union and yet spends hours on consecutive nights singing to Laura "like a lost soul" and following her by day "at a certain fixed distance around the Merced market through the Zocolo, up Francisco I. Madero Avenue, and so along the Paseo de la Reforma to Chapultepec Park, and into "the Philosopher's Footpath."[7] His movement is a superficial pattern only, however, because he has not the zeal or vision of the leaders whose names adorn the streets and parks of the city, monuments to the true revolutionary spirit. He begins also to write poems to Laura which he prints on a wooden press (why else but for wider distribution?), and Laura knows that his "unhurried" and watchful black eyes "will in time turn easily towards another subject." Another version of the same chivalric lover is seen in the attentions of the young captain who once had been a soldier in Zapata's army and who now channels his fervor into "amusing" ardor for Laura. He writes to Laura: "I am a very foolish, wasteful, impulsive man. I should have first said I love you, and then you would not have run away. But you shall see me again." The ideal they are expressing is neither tragic nor graceful but is the "most trivial" version of romantic love which Porter described as "the pretty trifling of shepherd and shepherdess."[8]

Braggioni is the professional revolutionist. He wages war for gain and not for idealistic commitment. But he acts the part of the idealist well. When "crafty men" whisper in his ear, "hungry men . . . wait for hours outside his office for a word with him," or "emaciated men with wild faces waylay . . . him in the street gate with a timid, 'Comrade, let me tell you . . . ,'" he is always sympathetic. He gives them handfuls of small coins from his own pocket, he promises them work, he tells them "there will be demonstrations, they must join the unions and attend the meetings, above all they must be on the watch for spies. They are closer to him than his own brothers, without them he can do nothing—until tomorrow, comrade!" Tomorrow of course will never come, for Braggioni is in fact cruel and unsympathetic and says to Laura, "They are stupid, they are lazy, they are treacherous, they would cut my throat for nothing." He says of Eugenio who has taken all the drugs that Laura brought him because he was bored, "He is a fool, and his death is his own business. . . . We are well rid of him." He also tells her that he himself is rich, "not in money . . . but in power, and this power brings with it the blameless ownership of things and the right to indulge his love of small luxuries." Braggioni is so far removed from the original revolutionary zeal that he cannot understand why Laura is involved in the revolution at all, "unless she loves some man who is in it."

This, then, is the death that was in the revolution. The heroic faith is not present in the "revolutionaries" who are left to carry on the fight. In this sense Braggioni, the shock-haired youth, Eugenio, Laura, and the Zapatista captain have all betrayed the revolution. They simply go through the motions of being revolutionaries but without the idealistic commitment. The failure of the revolution, however, is centered in the Braggionis, who consistently have been interpreted in a particular light. Bad as Braggioni is, he has been regarded by most critics to be salvageable in that he after all is moved to contrition and tears by his sad-eyed wife's washing his feet. Mrs. Braggioni, by the same token, has been regarded as a foil to Laura and as one whose capacity for love and forgiveness enables her husband to transcend his human weakness. Laura's view of Mrs. Braggioni as one "whose sense of reality is beyond criticism" has been interpreted to mean that Mrs. Braggioni is an ideal in the story. However, a more careful look at Mrs. Braggioni and at the feet-washing scene reveals that both she and her husband have misplaced values. Feminism was an important part of the revolution, and Mrs. Braggioni is active in the feminist movement. She "organizes unions among the girls in the cigarette factories, and walks in picket lines, and even speaks at meetings in the evening." The narrative voice adds, "But she cannot be brought to acknowledge the benefits of true liberty." The irony lies in the two meanings of "liberty," neither of which she accepts. She does not free herself from male domination and yet will not concede to Braggioni's freedom from fidelity. "I tell her I must have my freedom, net. She does not understand my point of view," Braggioni says. Mrs. Braggioni may be a feminist leader, but she is not a true feminist. It is significant that we never know her given name; she is known only as an extension, or a possession, of her husband. She is not dedicated to an ideal but to a man.

As tempting as it is to see Braggioni's tears as a sign of his redemption, the tears are tears of only self-love and self-pity. Braggioni's vanity is his most obvious trait from the outset; Laura listens to him "with pitiless courtesy, because she dares not smile at his miserable performance." Nobody dares to smile at him. "Braggioni is cruel to everyone, with a kind of specialized insolence, but he is so vain of his talents, and so sensitive to slights, it would require a cruelty and vanity greater than his own to lay a finger on the vast cureless wound of his self-esteem." "The excess of self-love" has flowed out, "inconveniently for her, over Laura." And it is evident again when Braggioni enters his own house and sees his wife weeping, as she has done every night since he left. He is filled with tenderness at seeing her love for him. That love he can understand. She asks him whether he is tired, and it is then that he burst into tears. "Ah, yes, I am hungry, I am tired." Tired? Braggioni can be tired only from "the labor of song." And hungry? Braggioni has not been hungry for years. Mrs. Braggioni, cast in the image of Mary Magdalen, has placed a poor substitute in a god's role.

Laura has betrayed the revolutionary ideal because she has refused to acknowledge the absence of honor and zeal among leaders such as Braggioni. She has protected herself against the reality of the revolution by protecting herself against feeling. Eugenio's total negation of feeling is the extreme of Laura's repression of feeling. It is that to which she is destined, if she continues her course. And therein lies an additional horror.

Laura the betrayer is indeed the focus of the story. However, Laura as the betrayer of the revolution because she brings no love to it, or Laura as the betrayer of herself because she does not allow herself love, or Laura as Eugenio's betrayer because she makes suicide possible seems inconclusive.

Moreover, the label that associates Laura with Judas Iscariot seems too strong, especially when her acts of "betrayal" are measured against those acts of "betrayal" by other characters in the story. The evidence that is cited as proof of Laura's self-betrayal centers on two elements in the story: Laura's "frigidity," symbolically grounded in her nunlike appearance and her "notorious virginity," and the dream at the story's conclusion, in which Eugenio's calling Laura "murderer" seems to hit its mark so directly that Laura is terrified of returning to sleep. Porter, however, does not intend to portray a frigid or even sexually repressed Laura. She shows a Laura who has simply withheld love, as "the incomprehensible fullness" of her breasts, "like a nursing mother's," indicates. In fact, the complete withholding of love has been Laura's protection against brutal violence from revolutionists like Braggioni, who swells "in ominous ripeness" but who will grudgingly honor the ideal of chastity.

Laura's withholding of love thus has a practical cause. But she has justified the withholding in two ways that defy rationality. She has displaced love on the one hand, and on the other she has idealized it. In her total commitment to the revolution, Laura has transferred libidinous passion into revolutionary fervor, as the conclusion of her scene with Braggioni illustrates. Braggioni asks Laura to clean and oil his pistol, and the dialogue between them as Laura "peers down the pistol barrel" is heavy with sexual imagery and illustrates a subconscious collusion between them that Laura already has dreadfully intuited. Braggioni has told her, "We are more alike than you realize in some things," and after feeling "a slow chill, a purely physical sense of danger, a warning in her blood that violence, mutilation, a shocking death, wait for her," Laura thinks, "It may be true that I'm as corrupt, in another way, as Braggioni, . . . as callous, as incomplete." In a parody of a consummating love scene, Braggioni speaks of the revolution as a process that engenders a new life. "No one shall be left alive except the elect spirits destined to procreate a new world cleansed of cruelty and injustice." He "strokes the pistol lying in . . . [Laura's] hands, and declares, "Pistols are good, I love them, cannon are even better, but in the end I pin my faith on good dynamite." Laura's response would be appropriate were she responding to a lover's sweet appeal. But the gentleness is in contrast to the content of her words. She holds up the pre-pared ammunition belt and says softly, "Put that on, and go kill somebody in Morelia, and you will be happier."

Laura shows no aversion to the phallic suggestions in the scene. But if she has displaced her sexuality in the revolutionary moment, she also has idealized it, as is apparent in other important scenes. Her "tender" feelings about "the battered doll-shape of some male saint whose white, lace-trimmed drawers hang limply around his ankles below the hieratic dignity of his velvet robe" point to an idealized phallic appreciation ("she loves fine lace") and show how her encasement of principles has removed her from the intimacy of human love in any form. The children she teaches "remain strangers to her." Indeed, she does not love *them*, but she does love "their tender round hands and their charming opportunistic savagery."

Both Laura and Braggioni have substituted revolution for love, or death for life, as Laura's sleep-filling consciousness deduces immediately before she slips into the dream. Laura indeed betrays herself insofar as she denies herself the highest human fulfillment, which love makes possible. The dream, however, is cited as evidence that Laura is also the betrayer of Eugenio, who calls her "Murderer" and "Cannibal." In most interpretations the dream is seen as combining the two forms of Laura's betrayal. In betraying herself by refusing to give her love, she also has betrayed Eugenio by being unable to love him. Her providing the drugs which he uses for his suicide also supports the charge that Laura has betrayed Eugenio by making his death possible. The dream is of course crucial to the resolution of the story's theme. It is important to remember, however, that the dream is created in Laura's subconscious with the symbols of her childhood religion and that it externalizes Laura's own fears rather than offering objective proof of Laura's responsibility for Eugenio's death.

In the dream Laura is called out of sleep by Eugenio and instructed in a parody of the words of Christ, "Follow me." When it is clear that he is taking her to the land of death, rather than life, Laura resists, saying she will not go unless Eugenio takes her hand. Eugenio is already dead, and instead of giving Laura his fleshless hand gives her flowers from the Judas tree, which she devours greedily. However, when

Eugenio calls her "Cannibal!" and says, "This is my body and my blood," Laura cries "No!" and awakes trembling, "afraid to sleep again."

The most important symbol in the story, the flowering Judas tree, reaches the culmination in the dream. Flower imagery in fact has permeated the story, although the only flower named and described in the story is that of the Judas tree. The children Laura teaches "make her desk a fresh garden of flowers everyday," and when they write "We lov ar ticher" on the chalkboard, they draw "wreathes of flowers around the words." Flowers are traditionally a symbol of the female archetype, and there is sufficient reason to believe that Porter was using flowers in this sense in "Flowering Judas." Once when she was discussing symbolism, Porter remarked that the rose "begins as a female sexual symbol and ends as the rose of fire in Highest Heaven."[9] And in a sketch she wrote about Xochitl, the Mayan fertility goddess whose name means "flower," she described the goddess of pulque as also the earth mother who "sends rain . . . and makes the crops grow—the maguey [from which pulque is made] and the maize and the sweet fruits and pumpkin."[10] Thus Xochitl in Porter's sketch is the Great Mother who both gives life and provides pulque, a drug.[11] If flower symbolizes the female principle as it is embodied in Xochitl, then one can easily see how Laura has betrayed it, just as Miranda fears she has betrayed it in "The Fig Tree." If we recall Miranda's refusing the figs, another symbol of the female principle, and avoiding the baby animals at the farm because she thinks she has "given" death to the baby chicken, then Laura's detachment from the children she teaches is more easily understood. Her betrayal of her female self is represented by her throwing a flower to the youth who serenades her, not according to the custom of the culture to encourage his "love" for her, but in contradiction to make him "go away." The flower symbolically withers in his hat as he follows her through the city for several days.

Trees themselves, as the centers of vegetative symbolism, are another archetype of the female principle, and in this story flower and tree come together ironically in the Judas tree, the tree of betrayal, when the description "Judas" is interpreted by Laura's discarded Christianity. The title and the dominant symbols in the story support the theory that Laura

146

is betrayer of the female principle more than she is of anything else, and it is the recognition of this betrayal that terrifies her, much as it terrifies the young Miranda of "The Fig Tree" and "The Grave." The symbolism is completed in the dream when Laura devours greedily the "bleeding flowers" which satisfy "both hunger and thirst" in an attempt to integrate herself with the flower. Laura as the carrier of drugs has fulfilled only one rôle of the Great Mother and has denied the more significant rôle, that of giving nourishment, or life. Thus, Eugenio's telling her, "This is my body and my blood," horrifies her because what she had thought was an act of self-nourishment is actually an act of murder and cannibalism. Her awaking "trembling" is as understandable as Miranda's beginning "to tremble without knowing why" when she discovers the blood on the dead baby rabbits and understands at some place of "secret, formless" intuition that she has participated in death rather than life.

When Porter was writing "Flowering Judas" as well as some stories in the Miranda cycle, she would have been in her late thirties and early forties and perhaps unhappy about her childlessness. Letters Porter wrote to Eugene Pressly while they were apart in 1932 hint at a troubled relationship that may have been caused largely by Porter's unfulfilled maternalism. In one such letter, after saying that happiness for the two of them "seems possible, if not altogether reasonable," she immediately adds, as if by association, "I had the damnedest dream last night." She then recounts a complicated dream in which she was a bystander who saw dead men, one with "a heavy cross of flowers weighing him down," and dead women "clasping newly born babies." Her sister Alice was in the dream with another baby, which was Porter's, and regarded Porter with a "censorious look on her face." She tells Pressly that the dream was "very sinister, mysterious and portentous . . . and yet without meaning." The elements of guilt, flowers, and death—particularly in the form of dead mothers who could not nourish their babies—indicated that the dream may have related in a profound way to the stories Porter already had written and some she was planning.[12] She later recorded the details of a similar dream from the same period; it included both her and Pressly as well as a monkey who was starving to death in spite of her efforts to find milk and food for him. She says, "The dream ended I do not remember precisely how or when, except that my uneasiness was growing and the monkey was shriveling up and lying in the palm of my hand almost perfectly still and silent. It was a very anxious and unhappy dream and very hopeless."[13]

The important flower symbolism in the story is supported by other symbolism, that of machinery and oil. In contrast to her concept of flowers, Porter consistently thought of machinery as life-negating, observing in "The Flower of Flowers" that "the world of evil is mechanistic," furnished with "the wheel, but not the rose." And she once told a former lover that she knew their love affair was dead when it became clear that he wanted them to "be machines . . . functioning with hair's breadth precision."[14] Laura senses this hovering negation, because she has a proper fear of machines ("I shall not be killed by an automobile if I can help it," she says) and a revulsion for them ("her private heresy" is that "she will not wear lace made on machines"). Braggioni's threat to Laura is suggested in imagery that links him to machines and particularly to the automobile. "His skin has been punctured in honorable warfare" ("puncture" is a word directly related to automobile tires), and when he asks Laura to oil and load his pistols, she "sits with the shells slipping through the cleaning cloth dipped in oil." When Braggioni sings, he cheeks grow "oily," and his smile is "suety." Thus his Sunday morning ride down the Reforma, the avenue that is dedicated to revolutionary vision and bravery, is highly ironic.

Machine and oil metaphors are particularly interesting here, as well as in "Hacienda," because they have specialized meaning to Porter that they could not have had to Faulkner, for example, who also used them as symbols of anti-life and anti-nature, notable in *The Sound and the Fury* and *Sanctuary*. Porter's arrival in Mexico City coincided with the explosion of the so-called petroleum problem. Because Obregón stepped into the presidency during the depression that was the aftermath of World War I, he was immediately faced with many problems that grew out of the worldwide economic collapse. The Mexican federal treasury in 1921 was drained by the need to support the numerous unemployed in Mexico as well as to send help and railroad passage to the thousands of workers who had gone to the United States only to discover that depression and unemployment were there also. Thus, prices of raw materials dropped sharply, and Obregón had to suspend production taxes on silver, copper, and lead. However, the petroleum industry during these same years was remarkably healthy (1921 and 1922 were peak years in the production and exportation of Mexican crude oil). In order to replenish the treasury, depleted by loss of taxes on other raw materials, Obregón cited and upheld Article 27 of the Mexican Constitution as amended by Carranza in 1917; it was essentially a decree that the Mexican government had full title to all the lands in Mexico, both surface and subsoil, and had the power not only to break up and divide among the Indians certain unwieldy landholdings but also to tax subsoil products. The oil interests were enraged and suspended operations, throwing another four thousand persons out of work.[15] A compromise between the oil companies and the government was reached in which the payment of taxes was linked to the redemption of Mexico's defaulted foreign bonds, and although it was a compromise that would plague the Mexican government for more than a decade, it did lead to the United States's recognition of the Obregón government in 1924.[16]

Because Porter's reasons for going to Mexico in the first place were idealistic, she felt an immediate aversion to the capitalists and to oilmen, it seems, in particular. Shortly after her arrival there she described to her sister Gay her association with "rich men who were clever enough, but smell offensively of money, and who wish to hold your hand and be a father to you—or rather, three fathers. And I tell one of them," she says, that "I am handsomely supplied with a perfectly spiffing father, and a brother beside, and a lover into the bargain, and I can only be a 'talking friend' to him. At which he sulks in his fat oil magnate way, and I order my favorite dessert."[17] Within seven months, she was able to write an incisive article she called "The Mexican Trinity," in which she analyzed the intricate relationships among "the great triumvirate, Land, Oil, and the Church."[18]

The crucial imagery in "Flowering Judas" is tied directly to Porter's experiences in Mexico, especially her research into primitive myths and her observation of the effects of machines and oil on Mexican society. The machine and flower imagery represent Laura's dilemma. The machine has been linked to the revolution because it was to free the peon from bondage, an illusion Porter elaborates upon in "Hacienda," but Laura's aversion to it is an instinctual female response to its anti-life associations. The dilemma represents Laura's whole experience in the Mexican revolution, a subject Porter had put away by the time she started the Miranda saga in earnest. But she retained the most universal theme from "Flowering Judas," fidelity to the female principle, and integrated it into "The Old Order."

☐ Notes ■

1. See Ray B. West, Jr., "Katherine Anne Porter: Symbol and Theme in 'Flowering Judas,'" *Accent* 7 (Spring 1947): 182–187.

2. See M. M. Liberman, *Katherine Anne Porter's Fiction* (Detroit: Wayne State University Press, 1971).

3. Barbara Thompson, "The Art of Fiction XXXIX—Katherine Anne Porter: An Interview," *Paris Review*, No. 29 (1963), 102–104; and "Why She Selected 'Flowering Judas,'" in *This Is My Best*, ed. Whit Burnett (New York: Dial Press, 1942), 539.

4. Undated notes, McKeldin Library, University of Maryland. Quoted with permission of Isabel Bayley, Porter's literary trustee, and the University of Maryland. Mary Doherty is mentioned in Drewey Wayne Gunn, *American and British Writers in Mexico, 1556–1973* (Austin: University of Texas Press, 1973), 171. See also Carleton Beals, *Glass Houses: Ten Years of Free-Lancing* (Philadelphia: J. B. Lippincott, 1940), 324; and Peggy Baird, "The Last Days of Hart Crane," *Venture*, 4 (1961): 36–38. Yúdico was Samuel Yúdico, a minor revolutionist.

5. *The Collected Stories of Katherine Anne Porter* (New York: Harcourt Brace Jovanovich, 1965), 93.

6. See Mark 14:15 and Luke 22:12.

7. Laura's movements through the city traverse the greater Mexico City area. All the landmarks and streets have revolutionary significance and stand as a reminder of how far from the ideal Braggioni and the current revolutionaries have fallen. The Zócolo means "foundation" and is at the center of the old city and surrounded by the National Palace. Here once stood the halls of Montezuma. It also is the center of the independence celebration every year on Septem-

ber 15. Chapultepec Park also has a long history in the social evolution of the city. See Leopold Batres, *A Historic Guide to Mexico City* (Mexico: Imprenta Mundial, 1935). Porter may have been referring to the Chapultepec Park footpath known as the Avenida de los Poetas rather than the Philosopher's Footpath.

8. See "The Necessary Enemy," *The Collected Essays and Occasional Writings of Katherine Anne Porter* (New York: Delacorte Press, 1970), 185.

9. See "Recent Southern Fiction: A Panel Discussion," *Bulletin of Wesleyan College* 41 (January 1961): 13.

10. See Thomas Walsh, "Xochitl: Katherine Anne Porter's Changing Goddess," *American Literature* 52 (May 1980): 183–193.

11. Walsh points out that intentionally or not, in the sketch Porter was confusing the attributes of Xochitl and Mayahuel, the authentic goddess of pulque. Walsh believes that Porter "chose Xichitl's name because in Nahuatl it means 'flower' and Xochimilco means 'place of flowers.'" Walsh, 185.

12. See KAP to Eugene Pressly, 23 January 1932, McKeldin Library. Quoted with permission of Isabel Bayley and the University of Maryland.

13. Undated notes, McKeldin. Quoted with permission of Isabel Bayley and the University of Maryland.

14. KAP to Matthew Josephson, 7 January 1931; the Beinecke Library, Yale University; quoted with permission of Isabel Bayley and Yale University.

15. See John W. F. Dulles, *Yesterday in Mexico* (Austin: University of Texas Press, 1961), 106–108, 166–167. Among Porter's papers in the McKeldin Library are six pages of typed notes (in Spanish and English) of petroleum data, facts from which she probably drew for her essays about Mexico.

16. The oil companies were defended by such persons as Joseph Hergesheimer and Evelyn Waugh, but Porter, B. Traven, and Carleton Beals were among the writers who protested the methods of the oilmen and the devastating effect on the revolution in Mexico. See Gunn, 78. In her essay "Where Presidents Have No Friends" Porter explains that "oil should . . . [have been] Mexico's greatest asset, but the Guggenheims and Dohenys have made of it a liability almost insupportable to the country." She goes on to describe the Doheny interests as the "most implacable of all Mexico's interior enemies" and "the source of eternal unrest." See *The Collected Essays*

and Occasional Writings of Katherine Anne Porter, 410. Porter's correspondence for nearly a decade shows a continuing interest in the oil problems of Mexico.

17. KAP to family, 31 December 1920, McKeldin. Quoted with permission of Isabel Bayley and the University of Maryland.

18. See *The Collected Essays,* 402.

■ JANE KRAUSE DeMOUY ■

"Flowering Judas": Psyche, Symbol, and Self-Betrayal

Katherine Anne Porter wrote often about personal freedom and its cost to women bred in a culture that valued them primarily for their sexuality and maternity. Porter knew that biology isn't destiny, but she also understood the truth that primitives understand: biology helps create psychology and identity, and women, seen from ancient times as presiders over birth and death, find expression in nurturing. Porter also understood the human need of women to create and assert their personal identities, a freedom made possible by the social upheaval of the twentieth century.

Since the social structure denies her both, most of Porter's stories focus on the conflict a woman experiences when faced with this psychological dichotomy. Some of her protagonists, naive idealists, simultaneously long for romantic love, while striving to build an autonomy based on personal talent. These women inevitably find that giving in to love means bearing children and expressing their power through maternity, not personality. Others make terrible choices, denying themselves affection, sexuality, and maternity for the sake of personal identity. Such denial, as "Flowering Judas" illustrates, is never simple, and can become a betrayal of self.

"Flowering Judas" reveals how this conflict, when internalized in the deepest psyche, results in emotional paralysis. What makes the story more compelling than most is the technical intricacy of its symbolic structure[1] and its use of that structure to portray the otherwise inaccessible complexity of

---

From *Katherine Anne Porter's Women: The Eye of Her Fiction* (Austin: University of Texas Press, 1983).

the protagonist's simultaneous but warring and often paradoxical psychological impulses.

Porter here creates a circle of symbols, all of which are interlayered with each other. For instance, on the surface, "Flowering Judas" is the story of an attempted seduction which is told in sexual imagery and incident—thus the story of the virgin confronting her seducer. It is also the story of the idealistic näif confronting political realities—thus the story of the corruption of purity of purpose. It is ultimately the story of a woman's recognition that her attempt to walk a thin line for the sake of integrity, autonomy, and freedom may be impossible because of the limitations inherent in a situation which is supposed to free her, as well as those in herself.

Each story element is separate, but each signifies the other. The revolution itself is the marvelous psychosymbol which incorporates at once physical violence, chaos, corruption, and its own set of rigidities, as well as the psychic presence of all these confusions in the mind of the protagonist. Laura is attracted to the revolution because it is both exciting and idealistic and therefore speaks to her doubleness. She attempts to control these impulses in the same way that the young woman in "Theft" does. She will hold herself aloof, hold out, say no. Her most obvious restraint is sexual, but she is more than a constricted virgin; she restrains herself emotionally as well as physically, and she does both to prevent the violation of soul as well as body.

Consequently, by understanding Laura's psychosexual position, one can better understand the paradoxical questions she cannot answer for herself—why she has committed herself to the revolution, why she participates so coldly, why she cannot run. It clarifies, too, the meaning of her nightmare, in which all symbolic elements coalesce in a horrible epiphany she cannot deny.

The complex elements of "Flowering Judas" communicate themselves so subtly and are so intricately interwoven that they are difficult to decipher and separate. At the heart of the story is Porter's familiar conflict—the struggle between life forces and physical or psychic death.

The broadest manifestation of this, the revolution, is also a struggle between idealistic purpose and physical reality. It is a war waged in the name of the poor and oppressed, made

154

up of hungry, desperate men who have abandoned their ancestral religion with its miracle-working saints and who now look to technology and the machine for salvation. Laura, who has not lost the habit of faith despite her disappointment with the Catholicism to which she was born, reflects the dissatisfaction of the workers with their lot in life and their idealistic belief in the possibility of millennial change.

On the other hand, she is different from them. Her passionless exterior and her repression of emotion and sexuality identify her as *norte americana*—among, but not of, the Mexicans. Her personal training and standards still characterize her and dictate her insistence on authenticity: she commits political "heresy" by wearing only handmade lace in a time and place where mechanically produced products are revered; and in a country given to dramatic flourish, she rejects the attentions of men who rely on costume and romantic convention to impress her.

Another reverberation of the life-death conflict is contained in the stalemated struggle between Laura and Braggioni which provides the plot line of the story. Braggioni represents the revolution, but he is also political reality. Since he embodies at once the revolution as a holy war and a vehicle for personal power and private gain, he is a perfect antagonist to Laura's impractical idealism and need to believe. His worldliness and obesity are the antithesis of her ascetic ways, and his coarse sexuality offends her romanticism and, of course, threatens her physical virginity. Through three interwoven layers of meaning run strands of sexual and religious imagery. Betrayal recurs like an insistent echo, and the flower motif highlighted in the story's title carries the whole forward.

In an interview with the *Paris Review*,[2] Porter described the *donnée* which gave her "Flowering Judas." A friend had asked Porter to sit with her while she was being visited by a man who intimidated her. As Porter passed her friend's window she saw the tableau created by the woman, the man seated with her, and the Flowering Judas underneath the window. Porter recreates that tableau through structure and use of language. Like "Theft," "Flowering Judas" is a two-part story, and, as in the former, Porter here skillfully encloses past history within the present moment. Laura, the protagonist, returns home in the evening to find Braggioni, the revolutionary leader, waiting for her as usual. She works for the revolution, but more specifically she works for Braggioni, to whom she owes her "comfortable situation and salary"; she may not turn him out, though his visits are threatening and distasteful to her. He sings to her; she eats her rice and pretends to read while he sings to her again; and so they have done for the evenings of one month. His presence, his singing, his conversation, their actions—all have been ritualized into a repetition which halts time and solidifies these characters for our perusal. Frozen together in the repetition of this evening that is like all the other evenings of this long, spoiled month, all the parts of their psyches exist in one eternal moment.

Written in the present tense, the story powerfully evokes the alert concentration of the conscious mind. Thinking of the past, we call the thought memory; thinking of the future, imagination. But catching the present moment is difficult; by using present tense, Porter manages not only to capture that present moment in all its immediacy, but to establish its intensity by calling up the complex psychological associations behind each action and each comment.

Braggioni and Laura exist together in time only because of the revolution, a state of chaos which both supports new life and causes death. As a couple they suggest elements of both. Braggioni's hulking presence, for instance, suggests all Laura's disillusionment with the revolution; it suggests the presence of other romantic suitors she has had and her rejections of them; but the complex associations he represents also include the presence of the children she teaches, the prisoners she visits, and the dangerous errands she runs, all at Braggioni's behest. Ultimately it encompasses her repression of her sexuality and her paradoxical attraction to and fear of death.

As others have noted, "Flowering Judas" is an intimate portrait of a woman in suspension.[3] Caught between the two poles of her "early training" and the "developed sense of reality" (read "cynicism") required by the revolution, Laura is like a tightrope walker whose inability to go either forward or backward necessitates a fall. In the meantime, she maintains a precarious balance, poised above a psychological abyss.

Any consideration of Laura illustrates that she is a walking paradox. She is a virgin with the body of a voluptuary. A woman who needs faith, she cannot believe. Having chosen the revolution as an ideological framework in place of her Catholicism, she must keep company with its cynical, self-serving participants. Wishing to run, she betrays herself by staying, seduced by the constant translation of the ideal she wishes to believe in into the vulgar reality she resists, which is symbolized by the insistent presence of Braggioni in her sitting room every night. She feels these dichotomies painfully: "She cannot help feeling that she has been betrayed irreparably by the disunion between her way of living and her feeling of what life should be."

"What life should be" is related to the "set of principles derived from her early training." She worships nobility, faith, and purity. Her image of a revolutionist sounds almost Christ-like: he should be "lean, animated by heroic faith, a vessel of abstract virtues." Her revolutionist should be passionate but bloodless. She is disillusioned with Braggioni, "a leader of men" who is a gluttonous egoist motivated by a love of luxury, power, and the pleasure he takes in killing. Why Laura is drawn to the revolution in the first place is something of a puzzle to her. "Uninvited she has promised herself to this place . . ."; she wonders about "the nature of this devotion, its true motives, and . . . its obligations."

First of all, she is undoubtedly drawn, in her "romantic error," by the "abstract virtues" she attributes to the movement. That much is obvious and provides a superficial answer. It is also obvious that she substitutes the revolution and its doctrines for the religious doctrine of her childhood. But there is something more. With her own emotions in turmoil, she must be attracted to the essential chaos of a sweeping change like revolution. At the same time, she attempts to control turmoil and change in herself; she is even rigid. Thus, her placing herself in a chaotic situation like revolution paradoxically indicates both a desire to be purged of rigidity—that is, to be different from what she is—and a desire for destruction of her old self.

The revolution has the same fatal attraction for her that a flame does for a moth. She is drawn to the light and heat of the battle, and particularly to the threat of death.[4] Even after she has discovered that being a revolutionary entails a daily round of mundane duties, "Laura feels a slow chill, a purely physical sense of danger, a warning in her blood that violence, mutilation, a shocking death, wait for her with lessening patience." Likewise, she has "uneasy premonitions of the future" and she practices stoicism "against that disaster she fears, though she cannot name it."

Which is not to say that idealism is not a strong force in her. That idealism holds equal sway with her is manifest in her religious devotion. She tries to resurrect the power of the Catholic faith she knew as a child; the value it had for her is caught in the image of the gold rosary she has bought in Tehuantepec. However, that power is disintegrating and false for her now. She goes to pray only in "some crumbling little church" where the beauty and richness of her faith has visibly decayed: the altar is decorated with "tinsel flowers and ragged brocades," and even the principals of this worship are ludicrous, like "the battered doll-shape of some male saint whose white, lace-trimmed drawers hang limply around his ankles below the hieratic dignity of his velvet robe."

If the stature of her religious faith has diminished, the ideal of purity which it has nurtured in her has not. Perhaps without realizing it, she lives the abstemious life of an anchoress. She has a celibate existence, with only one female servant for help and company; she spends her days and nights in works of mercy, teaching Indian children, visiting political prisoners, warning endangered rebels of the threat to their lives, and aiding their escape. When she returns home at the end of a long day, she frugally eats a simple plate of rice and drinks a cup of chocolate. She has "renounced vanities" and chooses to wear "the uniform of an idea": heavy blue serge dresses with confining, tight sleeves, and round white collars that are "not purposely nunlike." Braggioni wonders that she "covers her great round breasts with thick dark cloth, and . . . hides [her] long, invaluably beautiful legs under a heavy skirt." She has not only "encased herself in a set of principles," she encases her ripe sexuality in a restraining suit of armor. The only acquiescence to her femininity is the "tiny edge of fluted" lace on her collars, although even that has a pristine purity about it, since she will wear only handmade lace, which is therefore uncorrupted by machines.

She wishes everything about her to appear virgin. Among the Mexicans, her virtue is "notorious," since, for them, virginity is a state of arrested development. Young men pursue her, choosing to believe in the sensuality of her "soft, round under lip which promises gayety" rather than notice that she is "always grave." Braggioni himself lusts after her, refusing to believe that she is as cold as she seems. In his experience he has been pursued by both girls and married women, and although he scorns emotional attachments, the chase entices him. He cannot conceive that Laura has chosen celibacy:

> He cannot understand why she works so hard for the revolutionary idea unless she loves some man who is in it. "Are you not in love with someone?" "No," says Laura. "And no one is in love with you?" "No." "Then it is your own fault. No woman need go begging. Why what is the matter with you? The legless beggar woman in the Alameda has a perfectly faithful lover. Did you know that?"

She is such an anomaly—a cold virgin in a passionate land— that those who know her "cannot understand why she is in Mexico." Certainly, in an effort to retain her independence, she isolates herself, even from emotional involvement with the small children she teaches. Despite the easy affection they bestow on her, she thinks of them as strangers, although she has a sensual affection for their "tender round hands" and loves "their charming opportunist savagery." She is able to function so well as Braggioni's messenger because she keeps an emotional distance from prisoners and fugitives; any pity she has for them she keeps to herself. Because she has no sentimental attachments to the Roumanian and Polish agitators, they cannot exploit her.

While she thinks this stance is authentic, it is a masquerade that cloaks her subconscious desires; it is also a defense against herself. Just as Laura covers her ripe breasts with heavy cloth, restraining the sexuality she is afraid will burst from her, so she restrains her emotions, which keeps her from involvements whereby she might betray her values. She is not completely successful. Especially when she deals with romantic young men, she behaves guardedly, but an occasional inconsistency suggests some equivocation on her part.

For instance, the young captain formerly of Zapata's army has a noble simplicity about him that should appeal to

Laura. He comes close enough to her image of the ideal revolutionist that she agrees to go riding with him. However, he proves a "rude" hero, and he is not aggressive enough in expressing his affection for her. When he tries to take her in his arms, she spurs her horse, causing it to rear and gallop away with her. In actuality, it is she, and not her horse, who has become skittish. Laura's ironic tone in thinking about the young captain asserts that while first attracted, she has succeeded in rejecting him. Ultimately she mentally equates him and his affection with the children in her classroom, who brandish their emotions on the blackboard ("We lov ar ticher"), festooning the words with flowers drawn in colored chalks.

The romantic gesture of the youth who serenades her among the scarlet and purple blossoms of the Judas tree in her patio is appealing. It is the person she is not interested in. She tosses him a flower, on her Indian housemaid's instructions, only to find that he is enough encouraged by the gesture to follow her daily through the marketplace and about the city wearing the withered flower, like a dead hope, in his hatband. Significantly, Laura is "pleasantly disturbed by the abstract, unhurried watchfulness of his black eyes" which, as long as it is only a remote threat to her, is enjoyable. But the next lines are the most notable, for they reveal that she has not thrown the flower innocently:

> She tells herself that throwing the flower was a mistake, for she is twenty-two years old and knows better; but she refuses to regret it, and persuades herself that her negation of all external events as they occur is a sign that she is gradually perfecting herself in the stoicism she strives to cultivate against that disaster she fears, though she cannot name it.

Her understanding that she has encouraged attention by throwing the flower complicates the reader's knowledge of her, her gesture implies a willingness to entertain romance, but she is clearly unwilling to involve herself romantically. The tossed flower, then, is at best misleading, a tease whereby she flatters herself. She rationalizes that in her restraint she is building a strong stoicism which will defend her against "that disaster she fears." However, stoicism is not likely to protect

160

her from any other assault; stoicism will only protect her from herself.

Finally, there is another psychological reality in the slow chills she experiences in the presence of danger and in the pleasantly disturbing feelings here described. These are heightened moments of awareness for Laura precisely because danger is imminent. These situations must tempt her, or there would be no possibility of succumbing. It is the remote but implied danger which gives the moment its pique. Possessing a hidden but vital sexuality, Laura is also titillated by dealing in forbidden fruit. Like all good puritans, Laura know how to squeeze all possible pleasure from something she must not do, while at the same time avoiding guilt for having done it.

Nevertheless, perhaps because she suspects she is capable of undoing herself, she fears losing her virginity physically, emotionally, philosophically. This is the "warning in her blood that violence, mutilation, a shocking death, wait for her with lessening patience." This is "that disaster she fears, though she cannot name it." It would be simple enough to assume that Laura suffers from morbid fear reinforced by the real prospect of treachery during a time of political upheaval. However, we are told that "she is not afraid to knock on any door in any street after midnight, and enter in the darkness. . . ." and that "she knocks at unfamiliar doors not knowing whether a friend or a stranger shall answer . . . . , that she may walk anywhere in safety . . . [and look] at everything without amazement." She rightly fears most the evil in herself, and controls this by automatic rejection: "No. No. No. She draws her strength from this one holy talismanic word which does not suffer her to be led into evil." As long as she denies everything, she may look at everything without amazement. The unnamed disaster she fears is not the physical death it appears to be, but the death of her essential self or psyche. The disaster she fears so much that she cannot name it is the annihilation of her precarious sense of self through sexual experience, which in turn signifies destruction of her personhood and her spiritual integrity.

On the literal level, Laura has severed ties with her former home and can no longer identify with her family and its way of life. She has given up the easy role models of marriage and motherhood and life according to the norms of her child-hood community. What is left after she has rejected those fa-milial and communal roles is a fragile knowledge of her inmost self, whose defining marks are its idealism and its virginity. If she loses either, there is little left. Her cynical revolutionary comrades try to rob her of her idealism, and she resists by refusing "to surrender her will to such expedient logic." She resists "violence, mutilation [and] a shocking death"—which is simply another way of saying rape—by denial and repres-sion of the emotions that would make her vulnerable. This is not to say that Laura fears—or fantasizes—actual rape, but rather that on one level sexual intercourse represents to her a violation of both body and soul.

This sheds light, too, on the reason she does not bolt from her situation. Three times in the course of the story she thinks about running but does not: "Still she sits quietly, she does not run." Why? She rationalizes that she has no place else to go: "she can no longer imagine herself as living in an-other country, and there is no pleasure in remembering her life before she came here." Aside from the fact that this rea-soning overlooks the problem of why she chose to come to Mexico in the first place, it is obvious that she has deliberately cut herself off from her roots by placing herself in a culture so foreign to her own. She cannot go home, and she appears to reject going forward.

Like an initiate who has been cut off from her source and not yet assimilated into a new group, she exists in a state of potency which she seems to desire to maintain, rather than *become* anything else. She wishes to immobilize herself in time, like the figures on Keats's Grecian urn, to maintain the moment of anticipation by refusing to achieve it. By main-taining her liminal state, she can experience the tantaliza-tion of erotic pleasure without experiencing complete sexual knowledge and its responsibilities. Acquiring actual sexual knowledge is a dead loss in her own mind, as we have seen, and consequently she rejects that option out of hand. It does not occur to her that she might become something more than she already is through sexual experience; for Laura, it is death rather than metamorphosis. In fact, Laura is both attracted to and frightened by sex for several reasons. She has already re-jected her native country, the society in which she was born,

162

for the foreign one of Mexico because in her family's world anatomy is destiny. (This is certainly true for Mexican women, too, but Laura's position as an outsider releases her to some extent from the customs of the country for women.) Laura rightly understands that the only way she can control her life and exercise some autonomy of her own is by controlling her anatomy. By leaving her home she has eluded the necessity for marrying, bearing children, "settling down." Thus she has become something of a lay nun, a professional virgin. She can only respond with deviousness to the Mexican men who pursue her, and for the children she teaches she feels no affection, because men and children who offer her love require an emotional commitment and represent too closely the way of life she has rejected.

However, this assumed role presents her with various problems, both practical and philosophical. Having removed herself from the society in which she would naturally marry and become a mother, she has lost the simple and natural way of losing her virginity. A highly structured society like the one native to her at least provides a natural—and protected—framework wherein its women may pass out of maidenhood. Attired in her virginity as she is, and alone in the world, any change in her position must be ostentatious and scandalous, qualities her character cannot abide. She has, perhaps unconsciously, put herself in a position that precludes a sexual/emotional relationship, while at the same time she hungers for one—thus her precarious balancing act, midway between two poles of experience, and the sense of constriction and arrested development that emanates from her.

Aside from these practical considerations, a sexual act is not one that Laura could undertake casually, even if circumstances encouraged it. For her, sex is a symbolic act as well as a physical one (in this attitude she is a prototype of many other Porter heroines), for her sense of self is closely tied to her sexuality. Consequently, for her, learning to be a sexual creature is not simply a matter of learning how to use a part of the body, like learning to walk or hold a spoon. Becoming sexual, for Laura, is a matter of becoming another woman. While intercourse is an act of becoming, a union which generates new life, for a woman whose identity is tied to her sexual status, it is primarily an act of destruction. First of all, it destroys her

physical integrity with pain and bloodshed; but, more important, for Laura it destroys not only maidenhood, but the person
who was a maiden. After intercourse she will no longer be a
virgin, and if she is not to be transformed into a mother, like
Granny Weatherall, then what she will be is completely unknown, a psychological void that cannot be explored before it
is experienced. Consequently, although Laura is irresistibly
drawn toward sexual acts, she restrains herself because, for
her, intercourse constitutes a leap of faith into possibility—
which is at best the unknown and which may turn out to be a
bottomless pit.

Aside from the uncertainty lying on the other side of
that act, there is yet another threat Laura might face. In her
own mind, through intercourse Laura will at the very least
cease to be the woman she was and will become a woman she
doesn't know. Suppose this new self, released from her strait-
jacket, turns out to have an appetite for sex? Suppose the new
Laura has a consuming passion for sex that, once begun, can't
be stopped? In that case, she will certainly have brought chaos
on herself, a chaos impossible for her to control. It would also
be impossible for her to control, in Mexico, circa 1910, the
response of her body to intercourse. An unwanted pregnancy
would visit on her a final loss of control, with her body repro-
ducing itself, inexorably, against her will.

Of course, Laura's psychological attitudes constitute a
metaphor. She has ambivalent desires not only for her body,
but also for her personhood. Thus, in the revolution, she can
experience a proximity to chaos and danger which allows her
a doubly erotic kind of pleasure. Her participation in the revolution, but on the fringes of it, is a symbolic dabbling in sexual
experience and a remote indulgence of emotional idealism: in
short, a way that she can live her duality.

Then there is the matter of Braggioni, whose suit is
the most direct challenge to Laura's physical, emotional, and
philosophical stance. While others are merely foolish in their
romantic attentions, Braggioni's notice is dangerous and not
to be avoided by simple stratagem. He is both vain and cruel,
so that to cross him or derive him is deadly. A thousand
women, he tells Laura, have paid for the insult offered him by
the first woman he loved. Consequently, she "must resist tenaciously without appearing to resist." A strongly sexual man

and a womanizer, Braggioni is a rather sinister *miles glorio-sus* whose overweight body is not, like Falstaff's, comic, but threatening:

> He bulges marvelously in his expensive garments. Over his lavender collar, crushed upon a purple necktie, held by a diamond hoop: over his ammunition belt of tooled leather worked in silver, buckled cruelly around his gasping middle: over the tops of his glossy yellow shoes Braggioni swells with ominous ripeness, his mauve hose stretched taut, his ankles bound with the stout leather thongs of his shoes.

He is repulsive, fairly oozing the putrefaction of rotten fruit and jaded decadence. For Laura he symbolizes all the "reality" with which she has had to temper her idealism. He is a "professional lover of humanity" who "will never die of it." He is a parasite, grown fat on the blood of the workers; when his minions have served their purpose, he forgets them, leaving them to rot in jail or die of their despair. His obesity also embodies her own fear of loss of personal control.

Thus he is a mirror of all the things Laura hates and those she fears, too, especially her own propensity for evil. She worries that she may be "as corrupt . . . as callous, as incomplete" as Braggioni. Certainly she prostitutes herself by running his errands, for she is in tacit collusion with him. The taint of his corruption is bound to rub off on her, but "still she sits quietly, she does not run." Thus Laura, the unlikely revolutionary, idealistic but compromising, dissembles with Braggioni the killer.

Having established these several layers of meaning in the first part of the story through interior monologue, Porter braids them together for fullest impact in the climax. As in previous stories, she returns us to the present moment by repeating phrases which began the story and therefore reminds us that we are still attending that single moment:

> It is this month of separation for the sake of higher principles that has been spoiled not only for Mrs. Braggioni, whose sense of reality is beyond criticism, but for Laura, who feels herself bogged in a nightmare. . . . Laura has just come from a visit to the prison, and she is waiting for tomorrow with a

bitter anxiety as if tomorrow may not come, but time may be caught immovably in this hour, with herself transfixed, Braggioni singing on forever, and Eugenio's body not yet discovered by the guard.

The foreshadowing of Laura's nightmare is reinforced when Braggioni asks if she is going to sleep and then begins speaking hypnotically about the revolution, first in particular and then in philosophical terms. Almost every sentence highlights some motif of Laura's conflict. Braggioni emphasizes the dichotomy in Laura that is the center of the story when he tells her of the impending conflict between the Catholics and the Socialists in Morelia: "There will be two independent processions, starting from either end of town, and they will march until they meet, and the rest depends . . ." Inadvertently he describes the struggle between an irresistible force and an immovable object that is going on in the psyche of the protagonist.

Asking Laura to oil and load his pistols, Braggioni chides her for the absence of lovers in her life. As she fondles and lubricates his guns, Braggioni makes love to his guitar in the symbolic seduction which is the only rightful climax of this evening, to their month of evenings together. Laura says nothing, but what she feels as she peers down the pistol barrel recalls the quasi-fearful "slow chills" and the feeling of pleasant disturbance with which she responds to danger and sexual circumstances: "A long, slow faintness rises and subsides in her: Braggioni curves his swollen fingers around the throat of the guitar and softly smothers the music out of it."

Finally, in mesmerizing tones, as if chanting a ritual litany, Braggioni recounts the apocalyptic climax to the revolution, symbolically calling up the chaos and death of individuality Laura fears from intercourse:

> Some day this world, now seemingly so composed and eternal, to the edges of every sea shall be merely a tangle of gaping trenches, of crashing walls and broken bodies. Everything must be torn from its accustomed place where it has rotted for centuries, hurled skyward and distributed, cast down again clean as rain, without separate identity. . . . No one shall be left alive except the elect spirits destined to procreate a

new world cleansed of cruelty and injustice, ruled by benevolent anarchy.

"A tangle of gaping trenches, of crashing walls and broken
bodies" is not only an apt description of Armageddon, but also
a description of what a woman who fears the breaking of her
hymen expects to happen to her physically. Laura says good-
night by suggesting that Braggioni will feel better if he goes to
Morelia and kills someone. Then, made bold by "the presence
of death in the room," she confesses that she has failed to rescue Eugenio from his attempted suicide in the jail. Where
Braggioni will commit murder, Laura sins by omission; the
calloused leader refuses to be concerned and goes home to the
comfort of his wife. A third time Laura thinks that she must
run; a third time she denies her instinct and does not go, betraying herself.

As she drops off to sleep, burdened with the thought of
her betrayal of Eugenio's life and her betrayal of self, she sees
the children she teaches as prisoners bringing flowers to her,
their jailer. As her consciousness recedes, the warring con-
cepts in her psyche run together: "it is monstrous to confuse
love with revolution, night with day, life with death—ah, Eugenio!" In that passage to sleep and the unconscious mind,
Eugenio, the dead rebel, embodies her lost hope, her failed
nerve, and her stifled sexuality. He beckons her as demon
lover to accompany him to death; then, in a marvelous conjunction of images, sexuality, destruction, and betrayal rever-
berate against the life forces of nourishment, for both body
and soul:

> Then eat these flowers, poor prisoner, said Eugenio in a voice
> of pity, take and eat: and from the Judas tree he stripped the
> warm bleeding flowers, and held them to her lips. She saw
> that his hand was fleshless, a cluster of small white petrified
> branches, and his eye sockets were without light, but she ate
> the flowers greedily for they satisfied both hunger and thirst.
> Murder! said Eugenio, and Cannibal! This is my body and my
> blood.

In an inverted paradigm of the Last Supper, Eugenio offers
flowers of betrayal from the Judas tree, recalling the crucifix-

ion and his death at the hands of a betrayer. He appears at once as revolutionary, lover, priest, accuser, dead man, and death. He offers up his body and blood as a rebel willing to die for his cause, as a lover willing to use both sexually, and as a priest offering sacrifice. Laura accepts greedily, for he embodies simultaneously her hunger for both spiritual and sexual nourishment and her irrational compulsion to expose herself to destruction.

Much has been made of the superficial issue of Laura's betrayal of Eugenio, but her dream makes clear that there are many layers of betrayal in the story. First of all, it is Eugenio who entices Laura, not she him; and the apparent nourishment he offers is a stratagem. She is not deluded by him, since she sees that he is skeletal and recognizes that the food he presents is bleeding Judas blossoms. Since she is not taken in, when she accepts, she is not innocent but culpable. Eating greedily, she signifies her collusion and guilt and allows Eugenio to call her a murderer.

But her "betrayal" of Eugenio should not overshadow the far more significant self-betrayal which is the real stuff of the story. Aside from all the other things he represents, Eugenio is also a suicide, who first betrays himself. He is a rebel who has wanted a better life but who has not had the courage to survive. Thus he personifies at once the circular structure of Laura's psychic dilemma: her own idealism and death wish, her wish to participate in life even if it means death, and her simultaneous wish for survival at any expense—which, of course, necessitates spiritual death.

Thus Eugenio is the perfect embodiment of the maelstrom of conflicting desires which engulf Laura and prevent her acting, as well as the tangible evidence of the sin of omission she has committed in failing to prevent his self-destruction. It is in this last sense that he is most important in terms of Laura's psyche. Others—Braggioni and Laura—have failed to help him; but Eugenio's suicide has been first a betrayal of self.

And so it is with Laura. Betraying Eugenio, she betrays no one so much as her own person. Like the protagonist of "Theft," Laura is her own worst enemy, a woman who, in an effort to protect her integrity, has controlled her emotions to the point of being unable to act according to her own values.

168

In her nightmare, she confronts reality. By refusing to prevent Eugenio's suicide, she has murdered her own principles. In effect, she has become a suicide, too, a waking death-in-life figure whose image she tries to dispel by invoking her talismanic word: No. It is too late. In both body and blood, she has already raped herself.

☐ *Notes* ∎

1. The standard discussion of "Flowering Judas" is Ray B. West, Jr., "Symbol and Theme in 'Flowering Judas,'" *Accent* 7 (1947): 182–188; rpt. in *Katherine Anne Porter,* ed. Hartley and Core, pp. 120–128. West describes the intricate interrelationship of three "fields" of symbolism: Christian, mechanistic, and love symbols, which incorporate another triad—erotic, secular, and divine love. Leon Gottfried, "Death's Other Kingdom: Dantesque and Theological Symbolism in 'Flowering Judas,'" *PMLA* 84 (1969): 112–124, illustrates that Porter has drawn on *The Inferno,* T. S. Eliot's poems, and both Cassian and Aquinas in creating the characters, action, and imagery of "Flowering Judas."

2. Thompson, "Katherine Anne Porter: An Interview," in *Katherine Anne Porter,* ed. Hartley and Core, pp. 15–16.

3. This aspect of Laura's psychology is discussed in Sam Bluefarb, "Loss of Innocence in 'Flowering Judas,'" *College Language Association Journal* 7 (1964): 256–262. Bluefarb sees Laura as temporarily locked into the state of paralysis which automatically follows loss of innocence. But Sr. Mary Bride, O.P., "Laura and the Unlit Lamp," *Studies in Short Fiction* I (1963): 61–63, sees Laura's inaction as a denial of and refusal to participate in life. Dorothy Redden, "'Flowering Judas': Two Voices," *Studies in Short Fiction* 6 (1969): 194–204, comes closer to my view. She believes Laura survives only by maintaining equilibrium between dual forces in her life.

Porter herself elucidates and adds dimension to this issue in "Letters to a Nephew" (*Collected Essays,* 115). She appears to be describing Laura in discussing depression, which she equates with a general lethargy and unwillingness to act: "Psychologically, I believe it is supposed to have something to do with emotional and other frustrations due to inhibited libido due in turn to I forget what . . . firmly based on our hidden, long-denied wayward sexual impulses which keep us all feeling like criminals, or at least sinners. . . ." But what really interests her "is the theological view. It is called accidia or acedia, that is, Despair, and it is one of the deadliest of the seven deadly sins. All despair is, of course, in its deepest nature, despair of God's mercy, and you can hardly do worse. . . . my feeling is that the best thing you can do is say 'God be merciful to me, a sinner,' and try not to totter under your share of human perversity of thought and feeling." In other words, if one is to live, one must act.

4. One of Porter's most interesting pieces of nonfiction, "St. Augustine and the Bullfight" (*Collected Essays,* 91–101), dwells on the psychological fascination that apparently repugnant forms of excitement provide to even a reluctant participant-spectator, a discussion that provides insight into the complex character of Laura. The "earmarks" of adventure as Porter describes them aptly characterize the environment from which Laura cannot run: she is surrounded by "violence of motive, events taking place at top speed, at sustained intensity, under powerful stimulus and a willful seeking for pure sensation . . ." Furthermore, Porter might be speaking of her protagonist's psychological recognition at the end of "Flowering Judas" when she writes: ". . . adventure is something you seek for pleasure . . . ; for the illusion of being more alive that ordinarily, . . . but experience is what really happens to you in the long run; the truth that finally overtakes you." Again, Porter might be speaking in Laura's voice when she says of the bullfight, "But this had death in it, and it was the death in it that I loved . . ."

☐ THOMAS F. WALSH ■

The Making of "Flowering Judas"

Over the years Katherine Porter furnished many autobiographical details about her most celebrated story, "Flowering Judas" (1930), stating that "all the characters and episodes are based on real persons and events, but naturally, as my memory worked upon them and time passed, all assumed different shapes and colors, formed gradually around a central idea, that of self-delusion, the order and meaning of the episodes changed, and became in a word fiction."[1] This essay, drawing from Porter's published comments on the story, her unpublished letters, notes, and fiction,[2] and my conversations with her and with her friend, Mary Louis Doherty, attempts to distinguish between the "real persons and events" and the "different shapes and colors" they assumed. Despite the thin record of Porter's Mexican period, the questionable accuracy of her recollections of it many years later, and her reputation for fictionalizing her life, we can discover many experiences she transformed into "Flowering Judas" and the reasons those transformations took the shapes they did.[3] Thereby we gain a clearer picture of Porter's first year in Mexico and a better understanding of her creative process.

I

Porter's earliest comment on "Flowering Judas" appeared in 1942:

> The idea came to me one evening when going to visit the girl I call Laura in the story. I passed the open window of her

From *Journal of Modern Literature* 12, no. 1 (1985).

> living room on my way to the door, through the small patio
> which is one of the scenes in the story. I had a brief glimpse
> of her sitting with an open book in her lap, but not reading,
> with a fixed look of pained melancholy and confusion in her
> face. The fat man I call Braggioni was playing the guitar and
> singing to her.

Porter "thought" she understood "the desperate complications" of the girl's mind and feelings, but if she did not know
"her true story," she did know a story "that seemed symbolic
truth." In subsequent interviews Porter gave the expanded
versions of the "small seed" from which her story grew. In
1963 she added the Judas tree and identified the girl as her
friend "Mary" who was teaching in an Indian school and "was
not able to take care of herself, because she was not able to
face her own nature and was afraid of everything."[4] In 1965
Porter added the fountain and insisted that the small apartment where "Mary Doherty" lived alone was exactly as it appears in the story. Doherty, whom a young *Zapatista* captain
attempted to help from her horse, was a "virtuous, intact,
straitlaced Irish Catholic . . . born with the fear of sex," who
had asked Porter to sit with her because she was not sure of
the man coming to sing to her. This Porter did, outwaiting him
until he left in frustration. She refused to identify the man,
stating that she rolled "four or five objectionable characters
into one" to create Braggioni. She also claimed she was like
the girl in the story, taking "messages to people living in dark
alleys."[5] A few years later she added that she visited political
prisoners in their cells, two of whom she named.[6] In a lecture
taped at the University of Maryland in 1972, Porter gave the
fullest and least reliable account of her story's genesis, stating
that both she and Doherty brought food and sleeping pills to
political prisoners, one of whom persuaded Doherty to give
him fifty pills with which he killed himself. When Doherty
reported the man's death to "Braggioni," he told her they were
well rid of him. Later she dreamed that when she refused the
attempt of "Eugenio" to lead her to death, "he gave her the
flowering Judas buds." "This is her dream," Porter claimed,
adding, "You see, my fiction is reportage, only I do something
to it; I arrange it and it is fiction, but it happened." In a film
made at the University of Maryland in 1976, she stated that

Doherty should have known better than to give pills to the prisoner and, for the first time, gave Yúdico as Braggioni's model. As Porter added details about "Flowering Judas" over the years, reality more and more resembled what grew out of it, the story becoming "reportage," mainly of the actions and motives of Mary Doherty, about whom Porter could only speculate in 1942. Porter did indeed "arrange" reality to make it fiction, both in the creation of her story and in her versions of that creation. Her story is "based on real persons and events," but not as in her versions.

II

Porter met most of the "real persons" soon after her arrival in Mexico on November 6, 1920. She found an apartment on 20 Calle de Eliseo, next door to the home of Roberto and Thorberg Haberman. Although Porter never mentioned him publicly, Roberto Haberman, a member of the labor party instrumental in bringing President Alvaro Obregón to power, introduced her to the exciting world of Mexican politics. Porter wrote to her family that she was flattered to be accepted into an exclusive group close to or actually "the holders of the government reins." This group was to change Mexico and she expected "to be connected by a small thread to the affair." She also informed her family that she planned to write for *El Heraldo*, where Thorberg Haberman worked, and to collaborate with the Habermans on a revolutionary textbook. She participated in Obregón's inaugural celebration of November 30, drinking tea and champagne with him in his official residence in Chapultepec Castle, and also attended the lottery ticket sellers' ball in company with "the greatest labor leader in Mexico," Luis N. Morones, where she danced with "marvelous carbon colored Indians in scarlet blankets" until two o'clock in the morning. On Christmas day at the Habermans she met other labor leaders, among them her "beloved" R. H. Retinger.

Retinger, like Haberman, was advisor to Luis Morones. Working for CROM [Confederatión Regional Obrera Mexicana], he made valuable connections with international trade unionists in Europe and organized and directed Mexico's Press Agency. A participant in the League of Nations, an acquaintance of Gide, Mauriac, and Arnold Bennett, and a close friend of fellow countryman Joseph Conrad, he represented to Porter "Europe" in all its Jamesian connotations. In her notes she credits him with thoroughly educating her in international politics, but she never mentioned him publicly. They quickly fell in love, but the bickering that fills their letters is evidence enough that their relation would not survive their strong wills.

Mary Doherty, like Porter, was introduced to the labor group by Roberto Haberman.[7] At the Rand School of Economics she met Agnes Smedley, Thorberg Haberman's sister-in-law and later apologist for Red China, who encouraged her to visit Mexico. Doherty arrived in early 1921 and lived with the Habermans through July, briefly losing her bed to the legendary labor agitator, Mother Jones.[8] It was to the Haberman home that Samuel O. Yúdico came to entertain her with his guitar.[9] Doherty was soon assisting Retinger in his publicity work for CROM and teaching twice a week in Xochimilco, a few miles south of Mexico City. She traveled there with Yúdico or, occasionally, Porter and Retinger. Less self-centered and ambitious than Porter, more committed to Mexico's social progress, and, above all, more willing to serve in whatever capacity, Doherty became Porter's confidante and, in a correspondence that spanned fifty years, a continual source of information about Mexico. From the first, Doherty deferred to her more glamorous and talented friend, even rescuing pieces of writing Porter had crumpled up and tossed into the wastepaper basket. More tolerant than Porter of Mexico's shortcomings, Doherty still remembers incidents of her early days in Mexico with pleasure, especially the Sundays she and Porter spent in Chapultepec Park with their friends. She described the happy routine in a letter to her sister in 1921:

> We pasear in Chapultepec Park in a coche—those nice old family coaches with either one nice, sleek fat horse or two smaller ones with their clank clank on the pavement. Today being Sunday everyone passears from 12 to 2, the cars barely moving along—up one line and down another—much bowing, etc. You see everyone from Obregon down and since most of the people we know are gov't officials, they all come out in their cars—it is great fun.

(Porter also remembered those Sundays, for in "Flowering Judas" Braggioni "hires an automobile and drives in the Paseo on Sunday morning.")

On her first Sunday in Mexico, Doherty met Felipe Carrillo Puerto, then delegate from Yucatán and its next governor. She remembers him earnestly haranguing from a park bench curious passers-by on the glories of socialism. Porter first met him a few weeks before at the Habermans. They became close friends, often dining and dancing in Mexico City's nightclubs. Among Porter's papers are a description of the sinking of their rowboat in the shallow Chapultepec lagoon, his photograph inscribed to his "dear friend from Felipe," and a story he told her about a woman driven mad by the Revolution. Porter planned to visit him after he became governor in 1922, but Retinger discouraged her from making the arduous trip to Yucatán.

In January 1921, Porter and Doherty attended the convention of the Pan-American Federation of Labor. They both appear in a photograph of a large group of labor leaders, including Samuel Gompers, head of the AF of L, Luis Morones, Carrillo Puerto, and the Habermans. Porter describes in her notes a gathering of these labor people at the Haberman's house, where she fell asleep at the feet of William Green, Gompers's successor in 1925. According to Doherty, she and Porter were among those who saw Gompers off on his return to the United States, Porter contributing a farewell kiss. This was during the brief happy period of Porter's stay in Mexico.

III

The bright prospects Porter anticipated in December 1920 had evaporated by May 1921. She reveals her disillusion in "The Mexican Trinity" (August 1921) and "Where Presidents Have No Friends" (July 1922), the first essay beginning,

> Uneasiness grows here daily. We are having sudden deportations of foreign agitators, street riots and parades of workers carrying red flags. Plots thicken, thin, disintegrate in the space of thirty-six hours. A general was executed today for counterrevolutionary activities. . . . Battles occur almost daily

between Catholics and Socialists in many parts of the Republic: Morelia, Yucatán, Campeche, Jalisco.[10]

What follows in both essays is highly informative political
analysis, written from the point of view of one who firmly supports the goals of the Revolution, but hiding the fact that Porter herself deeply felt the growing "uneasiness." Her situation
evolved into Laura's in "Flowering Judas."

"Uneasiness" may understate the politically unstable
conditions of 1921. A clash between Catholics and Socialists
on May 12 resulted in the death of J. Isaac Arriaga, head
of the *Commisión Local Agraria,* which Porter lamented in
her journal, connecting it to the centuries-old history of un-
just seizures of Indian lands. His death provoked agrarian re-
formers to storm the Chamber of Deputies which became so
unruly that Obregón ordered the fire department to turn on its
hoses. Porter witnessed the hosing and reported it in "Where
Presidents Have No Friends." About the same time, Obregón,
complying with one of the conditions the United States stipulated for its recognition of Mexico, deported about thirty foreign radicals, among them several of Porter's acquaintances.[11]
Roberto Haberman was also on the list and went into hiding.
This incident frightened Porter, who recorded it many times
in her journal and letters, writing to friend Paul Hannah that
newspapers were clamoring for Haberman's head. She visited
him in hiding and described him sitting on a tumbled bed,
pale and drawn, and going over a long piece he had composed
about how Americans "crack the whip" over Mexico. Later
she began to turn this incident into fiction: "a certain Roumanian Jew agitator" recites "romantic yarns of personal treason" and composes a thesis against giving one man absolute
power. He resembles the "prisoners of [Laura's] own political
faith in their cells . . . composing their memoirs, writing out
manifestoes."

Even more frightening, Porter herself was on the deportation list. She wrote of rehearsing a speech she would
make to the police in order to gain time to pack. George T.
Summerlin, U.S. chargé d'affaires in Mexico, assured her that
her name had been removed, but another informant told her
later that it was not. In the meantime, her checks had been
held up, and for the first time in her life she experienced hun-

ger. She walked past secret service men sitting on the curb in front of the Haberman house, not caring whether they seized her because at least in jail she would be fed. Not finding Thorberg Haberman inside, she stole a dozen tortillas and a bowl of turkey mole. In another note she writes of crying a great deal and feeling sorry for herself: "Starvation is very hard on the flesh, and the idea of death is very hard on the nerves; I should like to deny that I am terrified but I am."

In a letter to her sister in June 1921, Doherty responds quite differently to the deportation crisis, giving in the process a rare, if brief, contemporary glimpse of Porter in Mexico.

> Of course all our crowd is on the list. . . . Bob [Roberto Haberman] is hiding with the papers yammering for his head. . . . Secret service people guard the house—all want us deported—Obregon would change his mind and cancel the order, but Americans keep up the rumpus and won't stop until they get Bob. It has been over two weeks now. . . . Strangely enough—no doubt due to the nervous tension and suspense—we who are still around loose are having a very good time—we go forth gayly with the leaders of the very government that has us on the list for deportation. Katherine, Thorberg and I have hilarious times. Of course we are really quite safe, for they won't take us until they get the more important ones and as yet we have done nothing because we can't speak Spanish—only in disrepute because of our beliefs and our associations and Katherine especially because she has refused to associate with the American colony. She is very pretty and very clever and they would like to have her and she is not very radical. . . . It will be very funny to laugh at a year from now—just now a little nervewracking.

This letter is not from somebody "afraid of everything," as Porter claimed Doherty was. Rather, the evidence shows that Porter herself was "terrified." In a note entitled "A month of uncertainties," she begins with the death of five followers of rebel General Lucio Blanco, adding "How on earth does this concern me? Yet it does." She then mentions the trouble stirring Catholics and Socialists in Morelia with "Yúdico and Bob polishing their pistols," the deportation of foreign radicals, Haberman in hiding, Summerlin's information, the hosing in the Chamber of Deputies, and finally her expectations of a summons any minute. At this time her friend Retinger was in the Laredo jail where she wrote him of all her troubles. In her recital Porter intertwines her own fear of deportation with deaths and threatened violence to others. The "uneasiness" in "The Mexican Trinity" is her uneasiness, tempting one to substitute her name for Carranza's in "Where Presidents Have No Friends."

Just as Porter mingles violence and death with her personal fears, so in "Flowering Judas" "the sight and sound of Braggioni singing threaten to identify themselves with all Laura's remembered afflictions and add their weight to her uneasy premonition of the future." Like Porter, Laura feels engulfed by the presence of death: "Laura feels a slow chill, a purely physical sense of danger, a warning in her blood that violence, mutilation, a shocking death, wait for her with lessening patience." And just as Yúdico and Haberman polish their pistols for "a row between the Catholics and Socialists . . . scheduled in Morelia for May 1st," so Braggioni asks Laura to "oil and load his pistols" because of "the May-day disturbances in Morelia." Out of her own remembered fears of 1921 Porter created the deathly atmosphere of "Flowering Judas."

With Laura's "warning in her blood" of "a shocking death" awaiting her, Porter gave full expression to her all-consuming theme. In this story, earlier fictional fragments, and later stories, culminating in "Pale Horse, Pale Rider," death is felt as a terrifying physical presence. In one fragment a character named Natalie complains, "There is something altogether horrible here . . . I am frightened of all sorts of things. I have terrible dreams," to which her friend Paul replies that he is "influenced by some indefinite thing in the air, a hovering and sinister presence." In "Hacienda" the narrator speaks of "the almost ecstatic death-expectancy which is in the air of Mexico. . . . strangers feel the acid of death in their bones whether or not any real danger is near them." Here Mexico is explicitly a place of death, symbolized by the "sour" odor of pulque, "like rotting milk and blood." In "Pale Horse, Pale Rider," the air is contaminated with influenza, infecting Miranda, who smells "the stench of corruption" in her own wasted body. This story was based on Porter's near-death struggle with influenza in 1918, but, she noted in her journal, she felt "the terror of death" stronger in 1921 than in 1918. When she wrote "Pale Horse, Pale Rider" in 1938, the terror she expressed had been magnified by her Mexican experience. Death is the firm link between Porter's Mexican and Miranda stories. She began the outline of the novel she was writing in Mexico with "Book I: Introduction to Death," which was to include Miranda's childhood. "The Grave" (1935) gives that introduction and tellingly ends with odors in Mexico triggering Miranda's childhood memories: "It was a very hot day and the smell in the market, with its piles of raw flesh and wilting flowers, was like the mingled sweetness and corruption she had smelled that other day in the cemetery at home."

IV

Porter's journal and letters give evidence that she viewed Mexico as a continual source for her creative writing. Seemingly nothing occurred that she did not weigh for its literary potential. She wrote local color sketches like "In a Mexican Patio" and "Teotihuacan" and recorded stories told to her by others.[12] But, as we have already seen from the deportation crisis of 1921, her main interests were the political and the personal.

Among Porter's papers is an outline of all the political parties in Mexico along with a thumbnail sketch of the leaders of each party. Her thorough knowledge served her well in such objective reporting as "The Mexican Trinity," but her ultimate goal was fiction. In May 1921, she wrote Paul Hannah of her "strangely assorted contacts" with diplomats, revolutionists, government officials, and unrestrained internationalists, adding, "I am making a story of these opposed forces." Elsewhere she recorded her intention of doing sketches of her revolutionary acquaintances, but what might have begun as reportage soon became "making a story." Thus Yúdico and Morones became Braggioni; Thorburg Haberman, Silberman; Carrillo Puerto, Vicente; and President Elias Calles, Velarde, the name Porter gives him in "Hacienda." The link between fact and fiction was her interest in the revolutionary personality, her estimate of which grew more cynical as time wore on.

Porter's personal experiences appear in her journal, often in the form of probing, guilt-ridden self-analysis, and in fictional fragments in which her alter ego Miranda makes her debut in scenes with her lover Jerome, who is based on R. H. Retinger. Porter intended to write "our story" about herself and Retinger, who was both political mentor and lover. Although she never completed the story, its fragments contributed, as we shall see, to the formation of Laura's personality.

Retinger himself influenced the composition of "Flowering Judas" in two different ways. While in a Laredo jail because of passport problems in May 1921, he wrote Porter to make sure that Luis Morones approved chapters of *Morones of Mexico* which she was editing. It is ironic that she, having read Retinger's adulation of Morones and Yúdico in this book, would eventually use both men as models for her negative portrait of Braggioni. Retinger wrote that "Yúdico, a tall, fair man, is a regular jack of all traces. . . . he knows every corner of the Republic, and understands the sufferings of the workers. Frank and outspoken, his equanimity is appreciated by his companions and his good heartedness makes him a friend of everybody."[13] Apparently Porter reserved Retinger's hollow rhetoric for Braggioni's followers who "say to each other: 'He has real nobility, a love of humanity raised above more personal affections.'"

Although Porter raised the thousand-dollar bail money for Retinger with an offer of five hundred dollars more and traveled to Laredo at the request of Morones to attempt his release, their love affair was fast disintegrating. In her journal she wrote that he would be pained to know how little she cared about his predicament. In later journal entries she described him as "an Austrian Pole much given to international intrigue" and "a complex and fascinating liar." In 1943, she still held a grudge against him, calling him, in a letter to Doherty, her "old enemy and parasite." No wonder her unflattering portrait of him in "Flowering Judas": "The Polish agitator talks love to [Laura] over café tables, hoping to exploit what he believes is her sentimental preference for him, and he gives her misinformation which he begs her to repeat as the solemn truth to certain persons." Behind this scene we can see Retinger professing his love for Porter in 1921 in the Café Colón on the Paseo, according to Doherty, one of their favorite meeting places. In the story, Laura is not deceived by the Pole's tactics as Porter felt she had been deceived by Retinger's. Reading the story, he would know that his former beloved had taken her revenge.

Porter also turned against Roberto Haberman, describing him in her notes as an unprincipled conniver who would practice any deception to advance his radical cause. In "Flowering Judas" he appears as the "Roumanian agitator": "He is generous with his money in all good causes, and lies to Laura with an air of ingenuous candor, as if he were her good friend and confidant."

As early as 1921 Porter planned to combine the political and personal in a novel called *Thieves' Market*. Through the twenties she added to it such events as Carrillo Puerto's death and Morones's fall from power. Later she conceived a three-book structure entitled *Many Redeemers* or *Midway of This Mortal Life*, which was to center on Miranda's whole life, beginning with "the history of the rise and break-up of an American family" and ending in the present with "the record of a rich and crumbling society." Mexico formed only a part of this grand scheme and was to appear as "the Mexican interval which is a tangent for Miranda, the complete negation of all she had known, a derailment up to 1928 or 30." The project would have challenged a Balzac. Begun in disconnected fragments, it ended as fragments of a much larger plan in the form of several short stories, "Old Mortality" coming closest to Porter's idea about the break-up of an American family. In the early thirties Porter visited Germany, which she apparently decided was more important than Mexico for the political statements she wished to make. The result was "The Leaning Tower" and *Ship of Fools*, according to most critics her least successful works, possibly because she was less acquainted with Germans than with Mexicans. But before turning away from Mexico, she did manage "Flowering Judas" to unite the political and personal. She quickly knew what she had accomplished, writing to a friend in April 1930, "It's by far the best thing I ever did and is in the mood and style of the novel." Although she continued to mention a Mexican novel in the forties, there was no need to write it, for her short story was the perfect distillation of everything the novel could have been.

V

The political dimension of "Flowering Judas," ignored by some of Porter's critics, is concentrated in the character of Braggioni. Since Porter did indeed roll "four or five objectionable characters" into one to create him, it is important to see how the revolutionaries she knew contributed to what was, in her jaundiced view, a portrait of *the* revolutionary.

A journal note dated 1921 begins, "Yúdico came in tonight bringing his guitar, and spent the evening singing for Mary." This early record of Porter's inspiration for "Flowering Judas" is devoted, as we shall see, to Mary Doherty with no other reference to Yúdico, but clearly he was the physical and moral prototype of Braggioni. The Yúdico who entertained Doherty was a tall, rather stout man with a fair complexion, light brown hair, and deep green eyes, sedately dressed with no pistols in evidence. His father, like Braggioni's, was Italian. Braggioni's "tight little mouth that turns down at the corners," giving him a "surly" expression, is an accurate, if unkind, description of Yúdico. Porter lightened Yúdico's hair, but turned his green eyes into "yellow cat's eyes" and his stoutness into "gluttonous bulk" which has become "a symbol of [Laura's] many disillusions" about how revolutionists should look and act. Porter's Yúdico was not the man Mary Doherty described as a friend to her family or the one Retinger idealized in his biography of Morones. If Doherty overlooked Yúdico's defects, Porter, as other journal notes suggest, saw nothing else.

Porter was apparently fascinated with Yúdico from the start. On September 8, 1921, she wrote of doing four portraits of revolutionaries, with his portrait almost complete. Also in 1921 she wrote that she heard Retinger talking with Yúdico, "a completely savage and uneducated Indian revolutionist, a man with the eyes of a cat and paunch of a pig and they both agreed that a woman was good for one thing." In a later note she advised herself, "Get into the scene . . . something of Braggioni's really sinister personality, the soft-spoken, hard-eyed monster." The shift here from Yúdico to Braggioni is imperceptible because Porter always saw Braggioni in Yúdico. Yúdico as sexual menace must have provoked her instinctive hatred. Another note begins, "Yúdico and his wife—went home to wash feet, wife came home sobbing . . ." and then continues, "Third Wife, fiftieth concubine—not faithful to anything. Study of Mexican revolutionary. . . . Given charge of blowing up and destroying Mexico City" if it falls into the hands of the enemy. Here and in "Flowering Judas" the sexual and political intermesh. Braggioni revenges himself on a thousand women for the humiliation one woman caused him in his youth just as he would brutally revenge himself against his political enemies if the need arose. His behavior is pointedly typical of the revolutionary who violates at every step the principles he pretends to uphold. In another note Porter wrote that the "spirit of revolutionaries is to escape from bondage to themselves. Their desire to rule, their will to power, is sort of revenge" to compensate for "their own insignificance, their sufferings." Porter, who attended a feminist meeting with Thorberg Haberman where she became the "79th member of the woman's party in Mexico," certainly viewed the attitudes of Yúdico/Braggioni toward women as a betrayal of the Revolution and a personal affront to herself and Laura.

In 1928 Porter shifted her attention from Yúdico, who died that year, to Luis Morones, explicitly identifying him with Braggioni in her notes. In 1922 she had praised Morones for paying munitions factory workers the highest wages in Mexico. With a thirty-million peso budget and a command of a large reserve of men, he enjoyed the prominence and power Porter attributes to Braggioni, with Retinger and Haberman, like the Polish and Rumanian agitators, contending for his favor. But Morones's reputation as a ruthless, corrupt politician became widespread. Porter's acquaintance, Carleton Beals, ridiculed him as "a big pig-like man . . . always meticulously dressed and perfumed, his hands glittering with diamonds."[14] In the same vein Porter described him in her journal as a "swollen labor leader . . . who removes inordinate silk scarf, and flashes his diamond like spotlights." He has "no higher idea that simple comforts and cheap elegance and direct forthright grabbing of whatever he can get." This description fits Braggioni with his diamond hoop and "elegant refinements" of silk handkerchief and Jockey Club perfume. When Morones's presidential ambitions made him suspect in the plot to assassinate Obregón in 1928, forcing him to resign his ministry, Porter wrote that he had done badly and used his fall from power to prophecy the fall of Braggioni, who "will live to see himself kicked out from his feeding trough by other hungry world saviors." In 1922 she had written in her journal, "if Morones is next president, salvation of Mexico is assured." In "Flowering Judas" words like "salvation" became bitterly ironic.

Angel Gomez and Felipe Carrillo Puerto, whose portraits Porter planned along with Yúdico's, also contributed to Braggioni's character. Gomez pops up in fiction fragments and plays a major role in "The Dove of Chapacalco," always as "the bomb thrower" or "the dynamiter"—for instance, "Gomez spent his time on knees as devotee, looking for chance to plan a dynamiting of the holy statue which is chief fame and revenue to church." A Cuban anarchist and member of the Federation of Workers, Angel Gomez was implicated in the bombing of a jewelry factory and in the invasion of the Chamber of Deputies on May 13. Porter probably met him at this time. She invests Braggioni, who pins his "faith to good dynamite," with Gomez's destructiveness. Braggioni envisions everything "hurled skyward" so that "nothing the poor has made for the rich shall remain." He would be more dangerous if he really believed his apocalyptic rhetoric which reveals his arrogance and hypocrisy since he enjoys the luxuries of the rich whom he would exterminate. To Porter he is the typical revolutionary, one of a "welter of small chattering monkeys busily making over a world to their own desires."

Carrillo Puerto did not live long enough to disillusion Porter, but her notes and financial fragments reveal her ambivalence toward him. He is the "beautiful bandit from Yucatan," "a dreamer of violent and gorgeous dreams," and "a complete dictator." His rhetoric, like Braggioni's, was radical, as were the changes he effected in Yucatán. He claimed direct descent from pre-colonial Mayan nobility, reminding us that Braggioni's Mayan mother was "a woman of race, an aristocrat." Porter's fictional name for Carrillo is Vicente, Braggioni's first name.

More importantly, Carrillo and others are the source of the ironic Christological imagery that unifies Braggioni's portrait. Critics are probably correct in assuming that the image of "Flowering Judas" derives from Eliot's "Gerontion," but the large pattern derives from revolutionary rhetoric. The photograph Carrillo dedicated to Porter had appeared in *Redención*

(Redemption), a publication of the Feminist League of Merida, Yucatán, the first issue of which (May 28, 1921) is among Porter's papers. Undoubtedly, socialists, opposed to a Catholic Church that, in their opinion, promised redemption to the poor in another life while collaborating with their oppressors in this one, reinterpreted Christian language imbibed in childhood and offered political and economic redemption here and now. Porter comments on the word in "Where Presidents Have No Friends": Best Maugard's "belief is that a renascence of older Aztec arts and handicrafts among these people will aid immeasurably in their redemption. Redemption—it is a hopeful, responsible word one often hears among these men" (Collected Essays, 414–415). But Porter's own hope vanished, and so Braggioni emerges as a perverse savior who, like Morones, only talks of "sacrificing himself for the worker." He is typical of *Many Redeemers,* which "is all about how men go on saving the world by starving, robbing, and killing each other—lying, meanwhile, to themselves and each other about their motives." Porter's description of her never-completed novel applies to "Flowering Judas."

It took nine years for Porter's views of several revolutionaries to blend and unify in her imagination. The result is the richly complex Braggioni, who is completely individualized in his brutal corpulence and perfectly typical of the revolutionary personality she came to despise. The process of Laura's creation is similar to Braggioni's, but complicated by the involvement of Porter's own personality in ways she may never have completely understood then or was willing to admit later.

VI

In her journal note of June 1921, Porter recorded her impression of Mary Doherty seated at a table, "a little preoccupied, infallibly and kindly attentive" to Yúdico as he entertained her with his guitar. She is "a modern secular nun," "a virgin but faintly interested in love," who "wears a rigid little uniform of dark blue cloth, with immaculate collars and cuffs of narrow lace made by hand." She thinks there is something "dishonest" in lace "contrived by machinery," but "pays a handsome price" for her "one extravagance." Born an Irish Catholic, "her romantic sense of adventure has guided her to the lower strata of revolution" where she "keeps her head cool in the midst of opera bouffe plots" and "submerged international intrigue." She intended to organize working women into labor unions, but does not realize that those who thwart her efforts are not as "clear and straight minded" as she. Although she has developed "a little pucker of trouble between her wide set grey eyes," she still "has the look of one who expects shortly to find a simple and honest solution of a very complicated problem. She is never to find it."

In her portrait of Doherty, Porter's selection and interpretation of details anticipates the creation of Laura. Porter saw Doherty, as she did Yúdico, pictorially, associating her "rigid little uniform" with her nunlike virginity (a uniform Doherty was still wearing in 1926, as Edward Weston's photographs show). That uniform will eventually symbolize Laura's fearful rejection of love in contrast to Doherty's dawning interest. Doherty's lace, like Laura's, is her one extravagance, but what she "thinks" about the dishonesty of machine-made lace is already a fiction in 1921, for she bought her lace at Altman's in New York, unaware whether it was handmade or not. In "Flowering Judas," Laura feels guilty about wearing the handmade lace when the machine is "sacred" to the revolutionist. From the start Doherty's dress had a meaning, but that meaning changed in the writing of "Flowering Judas."

Porter appropriated other details from Doherty's life to create Laura. Doherty's Irish Catholic background reinforced the image of "secular nun," although, unlike Laura, she was not a churchgoer. Like Laura, Doherty taught Indian children in Xochimilco, but never tried to organize women into labor unions. Her horse once ran away from a former *Zapatista*, Genaro Amezcua, who was head of the agrarian bureau in Cuernavaca where she first met him. Porter also knew him, describing him as "the only intelligent pro-feminist in Mexico," an ironic footnote to Laura's rejection of him and all other men in the story. However, such details do not account for Laura's personality. Doherty's honesty and genuine devotion to revolutionary reform, however naïve they seemed to Porter in her note of 1921, bear little resemblance to Laura's alienation and mechanical performance of duties in "Flowering Judas."

Porter's claim of coming over to Doherty's apartment at

her request to protect her from Yúdico is a fiction. Her 1921 journal entry gives no hint of such circumstances. At that time Doherty was not living alone, but with the Habermans. Also, she categorically denies that she was ever afraid of Yúdico, whom she described in a postcard in 1925 as "one of my good friends." Why then Porter's fabrication? Apparently she placed herself outside and inside the scene with Doherty and Yúdico. Outside, she imagined herself coming to the rescue of Doherty, who should have been afraid instead of sitting "infallibly and kindly attentive." Porter's account of outwaiting and frustrating Yúdico is a kind of posthumous revenge on him. Inside the scene, Porter identified with Doherty/Laura's "notorious virginity," expressing her own fear of violation in a world in which men were used to having their way with women. Porter treated endangered virginity in two other works of the period. The "dove" of "The Dove of Chapacalco" is a young servant girl who becomes the prey of a corrupt bishop. "Virgin Violeta" is based on Salomón de la Selva's account of seducing a friend's young daughter. Porter noted, "Salomón is uneasy because I told a friend of his I detested his attitude toward love and women—'If Salomón met the Virgin Mary, he would introduce himself as the Holy Ghost,' I said." And so she detested what she interpreted as Yúdico's advances on the Virgin Mary Doherty, in whom she saw herself, and fictionalized her detestation in "Flowering Judas." In this light Laura's notorious virginity is a positive virtue, other evidence to the contrary. Although it attracts Braggioni to her in the first place, thereby placing her in danger, it is a power she has over him. He can have his way with others but not with Laura.

Laura's virginity also has its negative side and partly explains why Porter chose not to name her heroine Miranda. Although the two characters resemble each other, there is a difference. Miranda is a woman victimized from childhood by circumstances beyond her control, from a family who does not understand her to influenza that almost kills her. If she has a fault, it is expecting too much from a world that always disappoints her, thereby justifying her reaction against it. Porter's criticism of Laura is much harsher. By insisting on Doherty as the original of Laura, she makes her friend the scapegoat for qualities she found difficult to admit as her own.

Negatively Laura's virginity represents total moral disengagement. She does not, understandably, love Braggioni, but she does not love anybody. Thus she is a traitor to the Revolution and to her own religious principles. Braggioni questions Laura's coldness: "You think you are so cold, *gringita!*", but his hope that she is not is vain, for she suffers from her author's own emotional problems.[15] In her journal Porter recorded Retinger's complaint that her "detachment from people and groups is a mark of her selfishness, is a sin against human solidarity." Another time he told her, "What you need is love. Your body will wither without it." Porter seemed torn between love and its smothering demands. After examining her attraction to Retinger, she concluded, "For I might as well acknowledge . . . love is not for me. . . . Love affects me as a great sickness of the heart, a crushing nostalgia that withers me up, that makes me fruitless and without help." In a fragment from *Thieves' Market,* Miranda "set herself perversely" against Jerome when he was "passionate," refusing to "respond" and feeling "happy in having spoiled his plan for him." Other times she was "really cold, as inaccessible as a virgin." Jerome would then call her "a Russian nun," telling her that she expected "to be taken as if [she] were the Holy Wafer." This fragment best explains Porter's ambivalent attitude toward Laura's virginity which is both revenge against Braggioni and symbol of her sexual and spiritual frigidity.[16]

Laura's spiritual malaise results in her guilt over the death of Eugenio. The facts behind this incident and Porter's visits to prisoners in jail are impossible to verify. Porter accused Doherty of supplying pills to a prisoner and of dreaming about his death, but Doherty firmly denies ever setting foot in prison until she visited photographer Tina Modotti in 1930, whereas Porter, in tears, told me that she herself had given sleeping pills to a prisoner who saved them until he had enough with which to kill himself, adding that only the death of the man who caught influenza from her had affected her as much. Porter's memory of her friend's death in 1918 probably contributed to Laura's guilt, but no corroborating evidence of visits to prison exists.

However, Porter did write of carrying messages that would result in the death of five men against whom she holds no grudge. She wonders if she is participating in "an act of opera bouffe treachery" out of boredom when she finally blames "the enemy within" her that "lives upon sensation" and "loves the sense of power implied in the possession of these letters" so "potent" that "five men will die at dawn" upon their delivery. This fragment may be Porter's fictional attempt to involve herself in the execution of five followers of Pablo Gonzales mentioned in "A Month of Uncertainties." Employing the present tense, it describes what she is about to do, not what she has done, and its language is melodramatic and calculated, "opera bouffe" repeating the expression she used in her portrait of Mary Doherty. On the other hand, it is in the first-person, like other autobiographical entries in her journal, whereas all the clearly fictional pieces of this period are in the third-person. If it is a true account of Porter's activities, then it explains the guilt she assigns to Laura, who also engaged in deadly intrigue she is not committed to.

Whatever the facts behind Laura's relation to Eugenio, her inability to love, deeply rooted in Porter's own personality, is directly linked to her fear of death, just as Braggioni's sexual aggression is linked to his deadly power. Such power Porter feared, writing in her journal, "Now I seem unable to believe in anything, and certainly my doubts of human beings and their motives are founded in a fear of their power over me." But fear of another's power makes love as dangerous as overt aggression and explains Laura's defense system. "Her knees cling together" as she closes herself to the "spread knees" of Braggioni, who fills her with a "purely physical sense of danger." This resistance is also seen in her escape from the romantic advances of the "gentle" *Zapatista* captain and the young typographer. But Laura's protective withdrawal into self only results in a death-like stasis of noncommitment. Her desire to escape perilous human involvement paradoxically leads her to the ultimate escape, suicide. We are told, "Sometimes she wishes to run away, but she stays. Now she longs to fly out of this room, down the narrow stairs, and into the street where the houses lean together like conspirators under a single mottled lamp, and leave Braggioni singing to himself." Here the urge to escape life ends in futile circularity, the conspiratorial houses a nightmarish substitution for Braggioni. This passage Porter developed from a journal entry in which she complains that she would "like exceedingly to die," not having "that sense of urgency" she had when she nearly died of influenza. Then she writes, "The streets are bowl shaped, and the houses lean inward . . . I have continually the sensation of stepping into space, and the side walk seems to curve down from the outer edges." In the next paragraph she predicts, "In a week I shall be dead." The leaning houses here are more explicitly related to suicidal impulse than they are in "Flowering Judas." It is as if Porter were viewing the world through a fish-eye lens, a world of unreal dimension she fears entering. In 1931 she wrote her father that she had struggled a long time "against the very strong temptation just to . . . quit the whole devilish nuisance of life," but now she was "in a healthy mood of resistance and energy." Only resistance applies to Laura. Throughout the story her "No" is a rejection of life, but her "No" to Eugenio's invitation expresses her rejection of suicide. She at least reaffirms her will to live despite her continuing state of irresolution.

Like Laura's personality, many of the story's details evolved out of Porter's own experience. For instance, the patio of "In a Mexican Patio," an unpublished sketch based on her experiences at 20 Calle del Eliseo, with its fountain and "purple" bougainvillaea, is the source of Laura's patio, with its fountain and Judas tree whose scarlet blossoms turn "a dull purple" in the moonlight. As evening falls, a young man appears as a shadowy presence, like Laura's young typographer, to communicate his love to a servant girl. Like "Flowering Judas," the sketch is narrated in the present tense and ends ominously at night: "In the sunlight one may laugh, and sniff the winds, but the night is crowded with thoughts darker than the sunless world." Journal entries supply other details. Porter's servant Maria was once "the prettiest girl in Guanajuato," the hometown of Laura's servant Lupe. Porter went to union meetings to hear the spell-binding Morones speak, while Laura goes to union meetings to listen to "busy important voices." In a fragment of *Thieves' Market,* Laura in church finds nothing to pray for: "Let me set my heart on something, I don't care how poor it is . . . the legless woman in the Alameda has a perfectly faithful lover—oh God, out of your charity send me something." Porter, who told me that she often saw the legless woman on a park bench sharing money with her lover, assigned Laura's lines about the woman to Braggioni and gave a mechanical "Hail Mary" to Laura, who is soon distracted by the "battered doll-shape of some male saint whose white, lace-trimmed drawers hang limply around his ankles below the hieratic dignity of his velvet robe." The saint originally appeared in "Teotihuacan" as "St. Ignatious Loyola with chaste lace-trimmed trousers showing beneath his black cassock." He is effectively denigrated by the transformation of "trousers" into "drawers." Clearly, "Flowering Judas" is based on Porter's own experiences, great and small.

VII

In 1943 Porter wrote Mary Doherty, "Mexico was new to us, and beautiful, the very place to be at that moment. We believed a great deal—though I remember well that my childhood faith in the Revolution was well over in about six months." By May 1921, the time of the deportation crisis, the prototypes of Braggioni among others had sufficiently convinced her that Mexico as potential paradise was and could be nothing but a dream. But out of the dreamer's failure came the artist's success. If Mexico could not assuage her troubled psyche, it compelled her to contemplate the entwined betrayals of Revolution and of self, and to transform her disillusion and spiritual isolation into Laura's. By donning, as it were, Mary Doherty's nun-like uniform, Porter was able to give voice to all her conflicting emotions and view them with dispassionate objectivity as if they were not her own. In later comments about the creation of her story, she persisted in her disguise, claiming that her friend was the model for Laura. "Flowering Judas" was not the "reportage" she claimed it was in 1972, but it did contain "symbolic truth" of her Mexican experience. Her transformation of purple bougainvillaea of her Mexican patio into flowering Judas is sign of the process that brought art out of life.

☐ *Notes* ∎

1. *This Is My Best*, ed. Whit Burnett (New York: The Dial Press, 1942), 539.
2. I am grateful to the McKeldin Library of the University

of Maryland for permission to examine Porter's papers and to Paul Porter for permission to quote from them.

3. For instance, Joan Givner, in *Katherine Anne Porter: A Life* (New York: Simon and Schuster, 1982), shows that the setting of "Old Mortality" did not derive from Porter's childhood, as Porter claimed, but from her stay in Bermuda in 1929 (211–213).

4. Barbara Thompson, "An Interview," *Writers at Work* (New York: Viking Press, 1963), 15–16.

5. Hank Lopez, "A Country and Some People I Love," *Harper's* 231 (1965), 59–60.

6. Enrique Hank Lopez, *Conversations with Katherine Anne Porter: Refugee from Indian Creek* (Boston: Little Brown, 1981), 119–120. Lopez first tape-recorded Porter's conversations in 1966.

7. Born in Iowa in 1898 and with a degree in Economics from the University of Wisconsin, Doherty served over the years in Mexico as secretary, translator, and researcher for various government officials. I am indebted to her for sharing her memories of Porter and for making her papers available to me.

8. Among Mother Jones's papers is Haberman's letter of April 1921, inviting her to Mexico where she traveled from mid-May until early July. See Dale Fethering, *Mother Jones, The Miner's Angel: A Portrait* (Carbondale: Southern Illinois University Press, 1974) p. 176–77, 247. This information helps verify Doherty's statements about her living arrangements in 1921, which contradict Porter's claim that Doherty was living alone when Yúdico visited her.

9. From 1914 to 1916 Yúdico was one of the ablest leaders and last Secretary General of *Casa Obrero Mundial,* which successfully organized labor syndicates.

10. The *Collected Essays and Occasional Writings of Katherine Anne Porter* (New York: Delacorte Press, 1970), 399. Subsequent references to Porter's essays from this edition appear in my text.

11. John M. Hart, *Anarchism & the Mexican Working Class 1860–1931* (Austin: University of Texas Press, 1978), 160.

12. In a note Porter listed Carrillo Puerto's and photographer Roberto Turnbull's stories of their experiences in the Revolution, both of which exist in rough draft, and Salomón de la Selva's "adventure with Palma's sister," which she transformed into "Virgin Violeta." De le Selva was a Nicaraguan poet, whom Porter, in her unpublished "An Encounter with Herman Goering," accuses of exploiting women, although he was "ingenuously charming and . . .

could disarm even most wary persons." She inscribed in her copy of Emily Dickinson's poetry "Salomón de la Selva gave me this book in Mexico City in 1922, after reading every poem in it to me."

13. J. H. Retinger, *The Rise of the Mexican Labor Movement* (Documentary Publications, 1976), 91; originally published in 1926 as *Morones of Mexico*.

14. Carleton Beals, *Glass Houses* (Philadelphia: Lippincott, 1938) 58.

15. Porter reported to Lopez that in Mexico she received "unwanted" attention from men "obviously disconcerted by her coolness. One of her . . . friends once told her that certain comrades considered her a very cold *gringita*. Selectivity was so often equated with frigidity" (*Conversations*, 121). Givner's account of Porter's frigidity indicates that the comrades were right (92–93).

16. Dorothy S. Redden, in "'Flowering Judas': Two Voices," *Studies in Short Fiction* 6 (1969), argues that one of Porter's voices "concurs in Laura's self-condemnation," while the other approves her "spiritual refusal to yield" (201).

◻ ROBERT H. BRINKMEYER, JR. ■

Mexico, Memory, and Betrayal: Katherine Anne Porter's "Flowering Judas"

In a 1926 review of *The Plumed Serpent* entitled "Quetzal-coatl," Katherine Anne Porter judged the novel as evidence for what she saw as Lawrence's failed quest both to understand the primitive mysteries of Indian life and to invigorate his own life with these mysteries. "It seems only incidentally a novel, in spite of the perfection of its form," Porter wrote; "It is a record of a pilgrimage that was, that must have been, a devastating experience."[1] Porter went on to describe Lawrence's pilgrimage, writing that he "went to Mexico in the hope of finding there, among alien people and their mysterious cult, what he had failed to find in his own race or within himself: a center and a meaning to life. He went to the Indians with the hope of clinching once and for all his argument that blood-nodality is the source of communion between man and man, and between man and the implacable gods. He desired to share this nodality, to wring from it the secret of the 'second strength' which gives magic powers to a man." Lawrence failed in his efforts, Porter argued, because he was too much a man of modern society; citing an observation of Kate Leslie, a character in the novel, that between the Indians and the whites lies "a wide space of neutral territory." Porter said that it was precisely this neutral territory that Lawrence could never cross, despite the tenacity of his will and the richness of his poetic imagination. In turning away from modern society and its neuroses, and looking instead to Indian ways for his soul's sustenance—Porter cites Kate's cry as an expression of

Lawrence's own quest: "Give me the mystery and let the world live again for me,' Kate cried in her own soul. 'And deliver me from man's automatism'"—Lawrence could not see that the despairs and problems of modern people were also his own. Lawrence, Porter said, could not "touch the darkly burning Indian mystery" because "he is too involved in preconceptions and simple human prejudice. His artificial Western mysticism came in collision with the truly occult mind of the Indian, and he suffered an extraordinary shock." For all his efforts to achieve an enriching communion with the Indians, Lawrence in the end "remains a stranger gazing at a mystery he cannot share, but still hopes to ravish, and his fancy dilates it to monstrous proportions."

Porter's interpretation of *The Plumed Serpent* and Lawrence's feelings toward Mexico can also be read as a striking evaluation by Porter of her own interest in and involvement with Mexico during the early 1920s. Although her quest to understand and draw from Mexican folk culture may not have been as consciously conceived or endowed with as much as mystical import as Lawrence's, nonetheless, like Lawrence, she had looked to the primitivism of the Indians as a means to shape her understanding of the world; her critique of Lawrence's failure to cross the "neutral territory" separating him from the Indians is, by this reading, also a statement of her own failure to do so. As "Quetzalcoatl" suggests, Porter by 1926 still looked to Mexican folk culture as expression of life's depths and mysteries, as a counterforce to the abstractions and mystifications of modernity. A passage from *The Plumed Serpent* she cited in her review, one that she said captured a mystical truth of Mexico, points to Porter's continued attraction to the primitivism of Indian life:

> Mexico pulls you down, the people pull you down like a great weight! But it may be they pull you down as the earth pull of gravitation does, that you can balance on your feet. Maybe they draw you down as the earth draws down the roots of the tree so that it may be clenched deep in the soil. . . . Loose leaves and aeroplanes blow away in what they call freedom. . . . All that matters to me are the roots that reach down beyond all destruction.

Significantly, the thrust of Porter's analysis is on the difficulty, if not the impossibility, of people of modern society ever experiencing fully the primitivist earth; like Lawrence, Porter appears to be saying, modern people carry with them too much social and cultural baggage that separates them on a fundamental level from Indian culture. Rather than knowing Indian culture—that is, of crossing the neutral territory separating modern and traditional cultures—moderns merely create a vision of the Indians of their own doing to fulfill their own needs. Such manipulation in representing primitive culture is precisely what Marianna Torgovnick finds endemic in the twentieth-century's confrontation with pre-modern societies:

> Those who study or write about the primitive usually begin by defining it as different from (usually opposite to) the present. After that, reactions to the present take over. Is the present too materialistic? Primitive life is not—it is a pre-capitalist utopia in which only use value, never exchange value, prevails. Is the present sexually repressed? Not primitive life—primitives live life whole, without fear of the body. Is the present promiscuous and undiscriminating sexually? Then primitives teach us the inevitable limits and controls placed on sexuality and the proper subordination of sexuality to the needs of child rearing. Does the present see itself as righteously Christian? Then primitives become heathens, mired in false beliefs. Does the present include vigorous business expansion? Then primitives cease to be thought of as human and become a resource for industry, able to work mines and supply natural wealth. In each case, the needs of the present determine the value and nature of the primitive. The primitive does what we ask it to do. Voiceless, it lets us speak for it. It is our ventriloquist's dummy—or so we like to think.[2]

Lawrence's downfall, says Porter, and I think her words speak more generally to the modern experience with primitive culture, is that "he turned soothsayer, and began to interpret by a formula: the result is a fresh myth of the Indian, a deeply emotional conception, but a myth none the less, and a debased one." Lawrence's Indians, she says later in the review, "are

197

merely what the Indians might be if they were all D. H. Lawrences."

"Quetzalcoatl" thus expresses the growing complexity of Porter's attitude toward primitivist Mexican culture—an attitude that by the mid-1920s was at the same time both celebrating Indian culture and questioning its relevance to the modern experience. Porter's questionings only intensified with time, so that by the late 1920s and early 1930s, and particularly after her return visit in 1930, her writings on Mexico—letters, reviews, and fiction—reveal her progressive disenchantment with the country and more generally with primitivism and its (re)vitalizing potential. By 1931, as revealed in a letter (11 November 1931) to Eugene Pressly, Porter had thoroughly revised her perspective on the value of folk culture and art to the modern mind; where she had once seen primitivist culture as a reference point—what Clifford Geertz calls a "conceptual center-point around which a comprehensive system of analysis can be built"[3]—she now finds such a perspective false, a posture, chicanery. Her comments come in a description of a critical survey of modern Mexican art on which she was then working; the survey, she wrote, was to be a "critical re-estimate" and "a firm but gentle remonstrance against the fashionable adoration of peasant and 'primitive' art, which I believe is a sign of debased judgement and pernicious aesthetic anemia." Her comments describing her work and the ideas behind it are anything but gentle. After acknowledging that much peasant art possesses beauty and value ("it exists in its own right and some of it has a wonderful quality"), she roundly attacks those artists who attempt to be "primitive"—that is, those who draw from and imitate peasant art even though that tradition is alien to the modern mind which first and foremost has shaped the artists' sensibilities. Bearing the brunt of her attack is "the easy and indiscriminate hurrah for everything peasant and primitive; the imitation, the attempt to impose dogma, the standards, the state of mind that went into these things." "It is impossible and highly undesirable," she concludes, speaking of modern people's efforts to recover the primitive understanding of reality. "To be primitive it is necessary to think and feel that way; all imitation is bad, all attempts to put on a state or mind, a tradition foreign to our souls, is just fakery. . . [.] This will lead to my protest against the whole present Mexican snobbish and artificial simplicity, from Diego on."⁴

Porter never published the essay she spoke of to Pressly, but in a 1929 review of Anita Brenner's book on Mexican art and artists, *Idols Behind Altars,* she critiqued the Mexican artistic renascence, focusing on its snobbish elitism and false simplicity. Porter pointed out in this review that none of the Mexican artists who profoundly shaped the direction of the renascence of Indian art was a true-blooded Indian; indeed, "the great renascence is a movement of mestizos and foreigners," almost all of whom had been educated in Europe and had returned to Mexico "with years of training and experience, saturated with theories and methods, bent on fresh discoveries." Their situation was very close to D. H. Lawrence's. The artists looked to the Indians for inspiration, and in so doing "adopted habits of thought, and adapted methods of working, and went, in the process, very consciously 'primitive,' imitating the Indian miracle paintings, delving among ruins, searching in the archives, attending Indian fiestas, using the native earths for their colors." And yet they failed to see that their understanding of Indian life and the primitivism they emulated had less to do with the dynamics of Indian culture than with their own desires as manifested in their theories, and thus their imaginations were never touched deeply by the Indians. Indeed so strong were the intellectual pretensions of the artists—pretensions they incorrectly presumed to have discarded in order to embrace "the darker profounder current of instinct"—that the Indians were effectively silenced by the very movement that was hailing them. "The non-Indians made the experiments and did the explaining," Porter wrote, noting that in their utter domination of the movement the artists in effect "shouted for [the Indians'] silence at the top of their lungs." Rather than actively engaging with the Indians, the artists "talked among themselves, compared findings, each defending his own point of view, and ended, evidently in confirming one another's discoveries in all essentials."⁵ Thus their movement was not a flowering, returning to her observation to Pressly, but instead was one of "snobbism and artificial simplicity."⁶ In part an attack on the artists' blindness and naivete, Porter's review also questions seriously the very significance of primitivism itself, suggesting that primitive folk culture may finally have little, if anything, to offer the modern person.

Porter's reoriented perspective on the primitive Mexican culture she had earlier so enthusiastically celebrated drastically altered the shape and thrust of her fiction. As several critics have noted, Porter's stories on Mexico written after 1928 are much darker and more forbidding than her earlier work, with Mexico less the place of simple truth and beauty, then the battleground of death and destruction. Gone completely are the prelapsarian world of "Children of Xochitl" and the affirmation of traditional culture as found in "María Concepción." Porter's subject also shifts from that of Mexicans and the tensions with which they struggled within their own culture to that of expatriates, outsiders to Mexican culture, and their attempts to "know" the mysteries of Mexico. None of these expatriates succeeds in his or her quest for understanding, a fact that suggests both Porter's awareness of the difficulties involved in such endeavor (one's perceptions are shaped by one's desires and preconceptions) and her disenchantment with the relevance of traditional Mexican culture to the modern experience. Not insignificantly, Porter for a while considered the title "False Hopes" for her story "Hacienda," an illuminating indication both of the delusions Porter saw plaguing expatriates and of the failure of Mexico itself to follow through with its revolutionary agenda.

Porter's finest story from this late period, "Flowering Judas," explores both dimensions of these "false hopes," focusing on the psychological struggles of a young American expatriate, Laura, to come to terms with her American upbringing and her Mexican present. As in her fiction set in the South, most significantly "The Jilting of Granny Weatherall" and the Miranda stories, Porter here explores the torturous task of acknowledging one's memories and integrating them in a healthy way into one's present outlooks and predicaments. To engage one's memory was for Porter not an act of passive recall or a submersion into nostalgia; it was, rather, an engagement with a mysterious and ever-changing realm of meanings we all carry within us, in a real sense an encounter with another and secret self. Walter J. Ong's observation, in an essay on voice and belief in literature, that a person's "own 'I' is haunted by the shadow of a 'thou' which itself casts and which it can never fully exorcise"[7] stands particularly relevant to Porter: for her this shadowy "thou" is a person's memory, and only by entering into an open and free dialogue with this secret self does a person mature and achieve understanding, both of the self and of the world. To ignore or repress memory is to limit growth and potential, for in doing so people close themselves off from the multiplicity of life's meanings, thereby consolidating their own already established and self-assured understanding of reality, an understanding rooted in the belief that the individual consciousness stands alone, without a secret thou, unified and self-sufficient. Likewise, to give oneself entirely to memory is to be imprisoned in the past, with one's present needs and desires utterly devalued in the face of an unchallengeable and monolithic order. Porter, in contrast, endorsed a dialogic relationship with memory—a relationship wherein neither the conscious self nor the self of memory stood finalized or unchallengeable; rather, they forever engage in a dialogue that challenges each to respond to the other, a dialogue of ongoing creation and recreation that never lapses into monologue or becomes so strained to be destructive.

Laura in "Flowering Judas" suffers from an unhealthy balance between self and memory. Although it is not absolutely clear why Laura originally came to Mexico—"Uninvited she has promised herself to this place" is all the narrator says—it seems apparent that on one level at least her journey represents her desire to free herself from her past. In all likelihood she was drawn to Mexico by preconceived notions of the romance and mystery of the country and its revolution. Laura's present unhappiness derives in part from the shattering of her romantic illusions. Symbolizing her general disillusionment is the revolutionary leader Braggioni, who is fat and cynical rather than, as she had imagined such figures to be, "lean, animated by heroic faith, [and] a vessel of abstract virtues." Even more disturbing for Laura, however, is her failure to live free from her past; her earlier life still haunts her, keeping her so firmly in its grip that she actively embraces it while at the same time seeking to repudiate it. "She has encased herself in a set of principles derived from her early training," the narrator writes, "leaving no detail of gesture or of personal taste untouched." For this reason, Laura wears only hand-made lace, despite the fact that to her revolutionary brethren such preference smacks of counter-revolutionary elitism, since "the machine is sacred, and will be the salvation of the workers."

Most dominant of the principles Laura carries with her from her upbringing is her Catholicism. Although she is no longer active in the Church and espouses revolutionary loyalties—loyalties that see the Catholic Church as the enemy of revolutionary change—Laura nonetheless still feels the pull of the Church; risking scandal, as the narrator reports, "she slips now and again into some crumbling little church, kneels on the chilly stone, and says a Hail Mary on the gold rosary she bought in Tehuantepec." But appeals to the Virgin fail to fulfill her needs ("It is no good," the narrator says of Laura's response to her prayers), and Laura concludes her visits not as a consoled believer but as a detached observer, "examining the altar with its tinsel flowers and rugged brocades, and feel[ing] tender about the battered doll-shape of some male saint whose white, lace-trimmed drawers hang limply around his ankles below the hieratic dignity of his velvet robe." That Laura repeatedly sneaks into Catholic churches underscores both her desire for faith (together with the structure and order that religious belief would give her) and her resistance to abandoning her previous beliefs, something her revolutionary brethren call for in their enthusiasm for building a new future. "Everything must be torn from its accustomed place where it has rotted for centuries, hurled skyward and distributed, cast down again clean as rain, without separate identity," Braggionni tells Laura, as reported by the narrator. "Nothing shall survive that the stiffened hands of poverty have created for the rich and no one shall be left alive except the elect spirits destined to procreate a new world cleansed of cruelty and injustice, ruled by benevolent anarchy: 'Pistols are good, I love them, cannon are even better, but in the end I pin my faith to good dynamite." Laura remains unimpressed by Braggioni's bluster.

Even if Laura cannot bring herself to embrace the spiritual dimensions of Catholic life, she nonetheless enthusiastically adopts aspects of Church tradition, stripped of their spiritual dimensions, to structure her everyday life. Most obvious and important is her rigid asceticism, a secular manifestation of cenobitic monasticism whereby the faithful, as Geoffrey Galt Harpham writes in *The Ascetic Imperative in Culture and Criticism*, "submitted themselves to extraordinary regulation, discipline, and obedience, living under a Superior in strict adherence to a Rule which prescribed their conduct, their attitudes, their food, and even their thoughts."[8] Such extreme asceticism, argues Harpham, ultimately entails the renunciation of self, since the ascetic "tries to live a life without content, without events" and seeks "not to be led into temptation so that the self would grow indistinct in its outlines, and would, ideally, simply cease to be."[9]

Laura, of course, does not live in a religious community, but she has structured her life around a renunciation of self and a rigid discipline that mediates engagements between self and world. Thus, even though she actively interacts with other people as a teacher and a revolutionary collaborator, she always maintains her discipline and reserve, resisting any deep commitment to another person, since such a commitment would undermine her life of denial. The narrator describes her situation:

> She is not at home in the world. Every day she teaches children who remain strangers to her, though she loves their tender round hands and their charming opportunist savagery. She knocks at unfamiliar doors not knowing whether a friend or stranger shall answer, and even if a known face emerges from the sour gloom of that unknown interior, still it is the face of a stranger. No matter what this stranger says to her, nor what her message to him, the very cells of her flesh reject knowledge and kinship in one monotonous word. No. No. No. She draws her strength from this one holy talismanic word which does not suffer her to be led into evil. Denying everything, she may walk anywhere in safety, she looks at everything without amazement.

Laura's rejection of others is matched by her rejection of her body. She denies what everyone else recognizes as her bountifulness, "cover[ing] her great round breasts with thick dark cloth, and . . . hid[ing] long, invaluably beautiful legs under a heavy skirt." When courted by Braggioni, Laura sits primly and rigidly, a posture that speaks of her discipline and her resolve to protect her chastity. The narrator writes that "she looks at Braggioni, frankly and clearly, like a good child who understands the rules of behavior. Her knees cling together under sound blue serge, and her round white collar is not purposely nun-like. She wears the uniform of an idea, and has renounced vanities."

Laura's asceticism pits her in direct opposition to Braggioni, who is driven by momentous self-love and -esteem. As the narrator writes, "Braggioni loves himself with such tenderness and amplitude and eternal charity that his followers . . . warm themselves in the reflected glow." If Braggioni was once driven by sincere commitment to revolutionary ideology calling for a more just world, he now focuses his energies on maintaining his power and in fulfilling his worldly desires. He is, as the narrator writes, "a good revolutionist and a professional lover of humanity"; that is, he acts with a coldness and a calculation that allow him to get what he wants and to get things done. "He has the malice, the cleverness, the wickedness, the sharpness of wit, the hardness of heart, stipulated for loving the world profitably," the narrator writes, and that profit is always his own, not others.' Braggioni relishes the trappings of power, and he indulges himself with free and easy abandon; despite the grimness of the times, he always has "good food and abundant drink" and plenty of women. "One woman is really as good as another for me, in the dark," he tells Laura. "I prefer them all."

Braggioni's comment on women underscores his self-centeredness and consequent lack of regard for other people— except in their capacity to serve him. When he is with the men whom he leads in the revolutionary struggle, Braggioni is always sympathetic and supportive, praising their efforts and promising them rewards, telling them that "they are closer to him than his own brothers, without them he can do nothing." To Laura he speaks of them quite differently: "They are stupid, they are lazy, they are treacherous, they would cut my throat for nothing." Braggioni may be right about his men (it is not clear from the story); but in any case what is significant is that Braggioni has no true "comrades," no one with whom he shares a bond not tainted with deceit and manipulation. This holds true even with his wife, from whom he demands fidelity and hero-worship, despite all of his own amorous entanglements with other women. "Unless you can learn to cry when I am not here," he tells her, "I must go away for good." Braggioni's abuse of his wife—he would lock her up, he says, if she ever proved unfaithful—derives not merely from the double standard toward sexuality that typifies relationships in patriarchal societies, but even more crucially from the self-centeredness and selfishness that fundamentally shape Braggioni's character and direct his actions.

In their manipulation of others and their commitment to noncommitment, Braggioni and Laura share a great deal, despite the fact that opposing drives propel their lives—self-denial for Laura and self-indulgence for Braggioni. Ultimately, both Laura's and Braggioni's actions embody a renunciation of human community, of the self in a world of others—and perhaps even of the world itself, since both place all value squarely within their isolated consciousnesses, thus emptying the world of value and significance in their quests to satisfy personal desires. Both Laura and Braggioni, in spite of all their differences, sense that they share this fundamental identity. "I am disappointed in everything as it comes. Everything," Braggioni says to Laura. "You, poor thing, you will be disappointed too. You are born for it. We are more alike than you realize in some things. Wait and see. Some day you will remember what I have told you, you will know that Braggioni was your friend." Laura refuses to see Braggioni as her friend, but she can't help seeing herself in him: "It may be true I am as corrupt, in another way, as Braggioni," she thinks, "as callous, as incomplete."

Eugenio's death severely tests both Braggioni's and Laura's ideologies of non-commitment. Braggioni does not want to discuss Eugenio's suicide or to accept any responsibility for it ("He is a fool, and his death is his own business," he says) because characteristically he focuses his energies only on his own matters and because, specifically in regard to Eugenio, he strives to deny any resemblance between his life and the prisoner's. Accepting this resemblance would undermine Braggioni's celebration of self, for Eugenio's separation in imprisonment from a vital human community and his discovery of the emptiness of a life focused merely on self-indulgence suggest similar failings in Braggioni's life; and his suicide points to the logical conclusion of a life directed totally toward pleasure when pleasure no longer fulfills. Adding to the pressure upon Braggioni is Laura's guilt about his death, her feelings suggesting a commitment to and a concern for others that transcend narrow loyalties to the self and that underscore what's missing in Braggioni's deceitful and manipulative relationships. Laura knows that his relationship with hers is of just this sort, and she taunts him by mocking his revolutionary zeal and his destructive interaction with others. "Put that on," she tells him, speaking of his pistol belt (his pistol is a charged image of the domination, sexual and otherwise, he seeks over others), "and go kill somebody in Morelia, and you will be happier."

Shaken by his encounter with Laura ("his mood had changed," the narrator writes), Braggioni does not follow through on Laura's derisive challenge, but instead returns home to his wife, from whom he has been living apart because he had found her not subservient enough. Braggioni's return to his wife and his tender treatment of her—"You are so good, please don't cry any more, you dear good creature," he says upon first seeing her—suggest that he now seeks a relationship not shaped by selfish self-love but by generous love for another. After his wife washes his feet, Braggioni is so thoroughly humbled that, as the narrator reports, "he is sorry for everything, and bursts into tears." "Ah yes, I am hungry, I am tired, let us eat something together," he says to his wife, inviting her to join him in a communion celebrating their love. Rather than tears of jealous anger, tears that Braggioni had earlier found so disturbing when he had left his wife, she now cries tears of joy that soothe and comfort, and suggest the beginning of a sustaining and giving relationship.

Eugenio's suicide likewise deeply stuns Laura, severely pressuring her ascetic life. Several forces impinge upon her. To begin with, feelings of responsibility for and guilt over Eugenio's death haunt Laura's consciousness (she carried Eugenio the drugs with which he killed himself and she did not call the prison doctor to save him), thoroughly disrupting her attempt to characterize all the people she knows as strangers, no matter how well she is acquainted with them. Ironically, it is only with Eugenio's death that he becomes alive to her—as a human being whose presence is entangled deeply with hers, rather than a faceless revolutionary with whom Laura has merely transacted business and who remains, to her eyes at least, completely outside genuine concern. Moreover, as it did to Braggioni, Eugenio's suicide speaks crucially to Laura's own predicament, a disturbing representation of her own suicidal turn inward into the prison of the isolated consciousness.

Not surprisingly, Laura is torn by conflicting feelings of guilt and denial. Despite her words to Braggioni suggesting their complicity in the suicide, Laura does her best, after Braggioni leaves and she rests alone, to repress all thoughts of her guilt; she is almost certainly aware of the disturbing implications to which her suspicions of guilt speak, implications that if openly accepted would almost certainly dismantle the structure of her asceticism. Not unexpectedly she looks to her ascetic discipline to maintain her stability; as she lies down to sleep, the narrator writes, "numbers tick in her brain like little clocks, soundless doors close of themselves around her." Despite this effort to close off the self from itself, Laura nonetheless fears sleep, for she knows she cannot control her dreams. She admonishes herself not to remember anything if she sleeps, and thinks ahead of the coming day in school rather than back on the day's events. Her efforts fail her: the school children remind her of Eugenio ("poor prisoners who come every day bringing flowers to their jailor"), and her attempt to count away her thoughts, 1-2-3-4-5, collapses in disorder, with the binary categories that structure her thought dissolving before Eugenio's image: "It is monstrous to confuse love with revolution, night with day, life with death—ah, Eugenio!"

The dream that follows works out her worst suspicions, looking backward to her complicity in Eugenio's death and forward to her own, as she departs with Eugenio on the journey to the other side of life. In an echo to the Last Supper quite different from that in the reconciliation of Braggioni and his wife (when she washes his feet), Eugenio offers Laura flowers from a Judas tree to eat and then himself becomes the very tree from which the flowers are stripped: "She saw that his hand was fleshless, a cluster of small white petrified branches, and his eye sockets were without light, but she ate the flowers greedily for they satisfied both hunger and thirst." "Murderer!" Eugenio accuses her, "and Cannibal! This is my body and my blood." Laura cries out "No!" in her sleep, and "at the sound of her own voice, she awoke trembling, and was afraid to sleep again."

Eugenio's stinging rebuke of Laura accuses her of betrayal—a betrayal not only of Eugenio but also of Laura's own self. Her interaction—or, better, her lack of interaction—with Eugenio is merely one manifestation of the life of denial she has so greedily embraced. Laura now comes to understand that her asceticism, bolstered by her stoic resolve, fails to nourish her in the ways she thought it would. Earlier, after a rash act that she refuses to regret, Laura, the narrator writes, "persuades herself that her negation of all external events as they occur is a sign that she is gradually perfecting herself in the stoicism she strives to cultivate against the disaster she fears, though she cannot name it"; but now she sees that her process of denial is less the means to perfect herself than it is to destroy herself—and also those about her. In her drastic turn inward that devalues the external world and her relationships with other people, Laura thus becomes precisely what Eugenio accuses her of being—a murderer and a cannibal, a person who sees other people merely as objects (thus "murdering" their selves, their humanity) to be manipulated in whatever way that will nourish her own desires (she thus "cannibalizes" them). And further, Laura's asceticism speaks to her own death and cannibalization; her isolation of herself entirely within her self is ultimately a life that feeds horrifyingly on itself.

As the narrator's words above suggest, Laura in part lives her ascetic life as a defense against an envisioned violent catastrophe that haunts her consciousness. But as she may come to understand upon waking from her nightmare at the end of the story (it is, finally, unclear precisely what Laura comes to accept about herself), the disaster she fears comes not with her death but with Eugenio's; and Eugenio's death, as we have noted, points to the catastrophe that Laura has carried with her all along, her destructive life of denial. In this Laura is not unlike John Marcher in Henry James's "The Beast in the Jungle" (Porter held a deep admiration for James), a man who commits his life to waiting for the disaster he foresees, the catastrophe, of course, turning out to be the very waiting itself, with Marcher destructively isolating himself from deep commitments with other people.

Laura's asceticism, as was suggested earlier, in large part derives from her inability to resolve the searching tension between her Catholic upbringing and her revolutionary present. Rather than bringing these two powerful forces into a constructive dialogue within her consciousness, whereby the two ideologies challenge and provoke each other and so become deepened and enriched, Laura instead brings them together for a destructive battle for utter domination. The tension thus lacerates rather than nourishes, driving Laura into inaction as she fluctuates between the two ideologies. She remains a traitor to both causes, the trace of one forever present in the other, so preventing her from giving full commitment to either. In the end she falls victim to her own inaction and denial, becoming as corrupt as the country in which she lives.

At one point in his wooing of Laura, Braggioni speaks of the violent disturbances upcoming in Morelia, where on May Day the Catholics and Socialists hold competing festivals. "There will be two independent processions," he tells Laura, "starting from either end of town, and they will march until they meet, and the rest depends. . ." Braggioni does not finish his story (or perhaps he does and the narrator does not report it), but the ending is clear: a violent conclusion to the day of festivities looms. Such violence arising from ideological conflict also rages within Laura; and so, too, does the violence at Morelia signify the disruptions that rage throughout all of Mexico, at least the Mexico of Porter's fiction of the late 1920s and early 1930s—a land torn to pieces by an internal war of competing ideologies, a land once of hope but now of destruction, a land run by people, revolutionaries or not, whose only conviction is to themselves and their individual welfare. Laura's confusion, despair, and suffering are Mexico's; the Edenic paradise of "Children of Xochitl" and "María Concepción" has become the wasteland, a land that has betrayed itself, a land of the Flowering Judas.

 Notes ∎

1. Katherine Anne Porter, "Quetzalcoatl," in *The Collected Essays and Occasional Writings of Katherine Anne Porter* (New

York: Delacorte Press, 1970), 421. All further citations of the review are from this edition.

2. Marianna Torgovnick, *Gone Primitive: Savage Intellects, Modern Minds* (Chicago: University of Chicago Press, 1990), 8–9.

3. Clifford Gertz, "Thick Description: Toward an Interpretative Theory of Culture," *The Interpretation of Cultures: Selected Essays* (New York: Basic Books, 1973), 3.

4. Katherine Anne Porter Collection, McKeldin Library, University of Maryland. The author gratefully thanks Isabel Bayley for permission to quote from this unpublished material.

5. Katherine Anne Porter, "Old Gods and New Messiahs," *New York Herald Tribune Books,* 29 September 1929.

6. Katherine Anne Porter Collection, McKeldin Library.

7. Walter J. Ong, "Voice as Summons for Belief: Literature, Faith, and the Divided Self," in *Literature and Religion,* ed. Giles B. Gunn (London: SCM Press, 1971), 71.

8. Geoffrey Galt Harpham, *The Ascetic Imperative in Culture and Criticism* (Chicago: University of Chicago Press, 1987), 21.

9. Harpham, *The Ascetic Imperative,* 29, 28.

❑ Selected Bibliography ■

Works by Katherine Anne Porter

My Chinese Marriage. (Signed "M.T.F"). New York: Duffield, 1921.

Outline of Mexican Popular Arts and Crafts. Los Angeles: Young and Mc-Callister, 1922.

What Price Marriage? Compiled and with an introduction by Porter (signed "Hamblen Sears"). New York: J. H. Sears, 1927.

Flowering Judas and Other Stories. New York: Harcourt, Brace, 1930.

Katherine Anne Porter's French Song-Book. New York: Harrison of Paris, 1933.

Hacienda. New York: Harrison of Paris, 1934.

Flowering Judas and Other Stories. New York: Harcourt, Brace, 1935. London: Cape, 1936. "Theft," "The Cracked Looking Glass," and "Hacienda" are added to the 1930 edition.

Noon Wine. Detroit: Schuman's, 1937.

Pale Horse, Pale Rider: Three Short Novels. New York: Harcourt, Brace, 1939. London: Cape, 1939.

The Itching Parrot. A translation of *El Perequillo Sarniento* by José Joaquín Lizárdi. Garden City: Doubleday, 1942.

The Leaning Tower and Other Stories. New York: Harcourt, Brace, 1944. London: Cape, 1945.

The Days Before. New York: Harcourt, Brace, 1952.

A Defense of Circe. New York: Harcourt, Brace, 1955.

The Old Order: Stories of the South. New York: Harcourt, Brace, 1955.

Ship of Fools. Boston and Toronto: Little, Brown/Atlantic Monthly, 1962. London: Secker and Warburg, 1962.

The Collected Stories of Katherine Anne Porter. New York: Harcourt, 1966.

A Christmas Story. New York: Delacorte Press, 1967.

The Collected Essays and Occasional Writings of Katherine Anne Porter. New York: Delacorte Press, 1970.

The Never-Ending Wrong. Boston: Atlantic-Little, Brown, 1977.

Letters of Katherine Anne Porter. Edited by Isabel Bayley. New York: Atlantic Monthly, 1990.

"This Strange, Old World" and Other Book Reviews by Katherine Anne Porter. Edited by Darlene Harbour Unrue. Athens: The University of Georgia Press, 1991.

Suggested Further Reading

BOOKS

Bloom, Harold, ed. *Katherine Anne Porter.* Modern Critical Views Series. New York: Chelsea House, 1986.

DeMouy, Jane Krause. *Katherine Anne Porter's Women: The Eye of Her Fiction.* Austin: University of Texas Press, 1983.

Emmons, Winifred S. *Katherine Anne Porter: The Regional Stories.* Southwest Writers Series, no. 6. Austin: Steck-Vaughn, 1967.

Givner, Joan. *Katherine Anne Porter: A Life.* Rev. ed. Athens: University of Georgia Press, 1991.

———. *Katherine Anne Porter: Conversations.* Jackson: University of Mississippi Press, 1987.

Hardy, John Edward. *Katherine Anne Porter.* New York: Ungar, 1973.

Hartley, Lodwick and George Core, eds. *Katherine Anne Porter: A Critical Symposium.* Athens: University of Georgia Press, 1969.

Hendrick, George and Willene Hendrick. *Katherine Anne Porter.* Rev. ed. Boston: Twayne, 1988.

Johns, Erna Victoria Schlemmer. *To Whom It May Concern.* Vol. 1: *The Schlemmers.* Austin: Privately Printed, 1975.

Josephson, Matthew. *Life Among the Surrealists.* New York: Holt, Rinehart, and Winston, 1962.

Krishnamurthi, M. G. *Katherine Anne Porter: A Study.* Mysore, India: Rao and Raghavan, 1971.

Liberman, M. M. *Katherine Anne Porter's Fiction.* Detroit: Wayne State University Press, 1971.

Lope, Enrique Hank. *Conversations with Katherine Anne Porter: Refugee from Indian Creek.* Boston: Little, Brown, 1981.

Machann, Clinton and William Bedford Clark, eds. *Katherine Anne Porter and Texas: An Uneasy Relationship.* College Station: Texas A & M University Press, 1990.

Mooney, Harry John, Jr. *The Fiction and Criticism of Katherine Anne Porter.* University of Pittsburgh Critical Essays in English and American Literature Series. Pittsburgh: University of Pittsburgh Press, 1962.

Nance, William L. *Katherine Anne Porter and the Art of Rejection.* Chapel Hill: University of North Carolina Press, 1964.

Stout, Janis P. *Strategies of Reticence: Silence and Meaning in the Works of Jane Austen, Willa Cather, Katherine Anne Porter, and Joan Didion.* Charlottesville: University Press of Virginia, 1990.

Unrue, Darlene Harbour. *Truth and Vision in Katherine Anne Porter's Fiction.* Athens: University of Georgia Press, 1985.

———. *Understanding Katherine Anne Porter.* Columbia: University of South Carolina Press, 1988.

Waldrip, Louise and Shirley Ann Bauer. *A Bibliography of the Works of Kath-*

erine Anne Porter and A Bibliography of the Criticism of the Works of Katherine Anne Porter. Metuchen: Scarecrow, 1969.

Warren, Robert Penn, ed. Katherine Anne Porter: A Collection of Critical Essays. Twentieth Century Views Series. Englewood Cliffs: Prentice, 1979.

ARTICLES

Bluefarb, Sam. "Loss of Innocence in 'Flowering Judas.'" College Language Association Journal 7 (March 1964): 256–262.

Bride, Sister Mary. "Laura and the Unlit Lamp." Studies in Short Fiction 1 (1963): 61–63.

Brinkmeyer, Robert H., Jr. "'Endless Remembering': The Artistic Vision of Katherine Anne Porter." Mississippi Quarterly 40 (Winter 1986–1987): 5–19.

Brooks, Cleanth. "The Woman and Artist I Knew." Katherine Anne Porter and Texas: An Uneasy Relationship. Clinton Machann and William Bedford Clark, eds. College Station: Texas A & M University Press, 1990.

———. "The Southern Temper." A Shaping Joy: Studies in the Writer's Craft. New York: Harcourt Brace Jovanovich, 1971. 205–208; 218–219.

Bufkin, E. C. "An Open Mind Profile: Katherine Anne Porter Talks with Glenway Wescott and Eric F. Goldman." Georgia Review (Winter 1987): 769–795.

Christensen, Peter C. "Katherine Anne Porter's 'Flowering Judas' and D. H. Lawrence's The Plumed Serpent: Contrasting Visions of Women in the Mexican Revolution." South Atlantic Review 56 (January 1991): 35–46.

Fetterley, Judith. "The Struggle for Authenticity: Growing Up Female in The Old Order." Kate Chopin Newsletter 2 (1976): 11–19.

Flanders, Jane. "Katherine Anne Porter and the Ordeal of Southern Womanhood." Southern Literary Journal 9 (1976): 47–60.

Gordon, Caroline. "Katherine Anne Porter and the ICM." Harper's 229 (November 1964): 146–148.

Gross, Beverly. "The Poetic Narrative: A Reading of 'Flowering Judas.'" Style 2 (1968): 129–139.

Hamovitch, Mitzi Berger. "Today and Yesterday: Letters from Katherine Anne Porter." The Centennial Review 27 (Fall 1983): 278–287.

Hicks, Granville. "A Tradition of Storytelling." Saturday Review 48 (no. 25, September 1965): 35–36.

Herbst, Josephine. "Miss Porter and Miss Stein." Partisan Review 15 (1948): 568–572.

Jones, A. G. "Gender and the Great War—The Case of Faulkner and Porter." Women's Studies 13 (No. 1–2, 1986): 135–148.

Lavers, Norman. "'Flowering Judas' and the Failure of Amour Courtois." Studies in Short Fiction 28 (1991): 77–82.

Nance, William L. "Katherine Anne Porter and Mexico." Southwest Review 55 (no. 2, 1970): 143–153.

Partridge, Colin. "'My Familiar Country': An Image of Mexico in the Work of Katherine Anne Porter." *Studies in Short Fiction* 7 (Fall 1970): 597–614.

Redden, Dorothy. "'Flowering Judas': Two Voices." *Studies in Short Fiction* 6 (1969): 194–204.

Scott, Shirley Clay. "Origins of Power in the Fiction of Katherine Anne Porter." *Journal of Evolutionary Psychology* 7 (March 1986): 46–56.

Sutherland, Donald. "Ole Woman River: A Correspondence with Katherine Anne Porter." *Saturday Review* 74 (Summer 1966): 754–767.

Tate, Allen. "A New Star" (review of "Flowering Judas"). *Nation* 131 (October 1930): 352–353.

Vukmirovich, John. "Porter's 'Flowering Judas' and Pynchon's *V.*" *Pynchon Notes* 22–23 (Spring–Fall 1988): 71–74.

Walsh, Thomas F. "Braggioni's Songs in 'Flowering Judas.'" *College Literature* 12 (Spring 1985): 147–152.

———. "Xochitl: Katherine Anne Porter's Changing Goddess." *American Literature* 52 (1980): 183–193.

———. "Identifying A Sketch by Katherine Anne Porter." *Journal of Modern Literature* 7 (1979): 555–561.

Walter, James. "Revolution and Time: Laura in 'Flowering Judas.'" *Renascence* 38 (Autumn 1985): 26–38.

Welty, Eudora. "My Introduction to Katherine Anne Porter." *Georgia Review* 44 (Spring–Summer 1990): 13–27.

Wiesenfarth, Joseph. "Negatives of Hope: A Reading of Katherine Anne Porter." *Renascence* 25 (Winter 1973): 85–94.

☐ Permissions ■

ern Literature 12, no. 1 (1985). Reprinted by permission of Thomas F. Walsh and *Journal of Modern Literature,* Temple University.

"Mexico, Memory, and Betrayal: Katherine Anne Porter's 'Flowering Judas'" by Robert H. Brinkmeyer. Reprinted by permission of Robert Brinkmeyer from his forthcoming book, and of Isabel Bayley, literary trustee for Katherine Anne Porter.